CLOSE
THE DEAL

Thank you
Tim

A. Sinccard

CLOSING THE DEAL
THE AL SINCLAIR WAY

AL SINCLAIR

BURMANBOOKS

Published by BurmanBooks Inc.
260 Queens Quay West
Suite 1102
Toronto, Ontario
Canada M5J 2N3

Design: Jack Steiner
Editor: Drew Tapley
Cover: Diane Kolar

Distribution:
Innovative Logistics LLC
575 Prospect Street, Suite 301
Lakewood, NJ 08701

ISBN: 978-1-927005-00-2

Table of Contents

Introduction

Over twenty-five years ago, I had purchased over ninety investment properties (owned forty at one time) and was well on my way to a multi-million-dollar empire. I was only in my mid twenties, and the glass was not only half full, it was full and spilling over.

I was not an agent then, and entrusted my real estate agent one hundred percent. He knew he had my trust, and I even purchased properties as sight unseen. In 1986, my agent made over $600,000 off my transactions alone. On our last purchase together, I bought a North York bungalow, conveniently owned by one of his clients and his lawyer. The purchase price was $351,000. No problem, just another deal. Well, there was one problem. It only appraised at $250,000. I confronted my agent about this, and he explained to me about how bank appraisals are always low. Maybe five or ten grand, I thought... but not $100,000. You see, I got buried (a real estate investor's term for being ripped off), and I swore it would not happen again, to me or to anyone I cared about.

I started my real estate career the next day in a classroom, and a couple of months later I was licenced. I swore that I would make my real estate career an honest and ethical one. You see, if my agent had not gotten greedy, he might still be making money off me today.

The knowledge that I amassed throughout my investment years was incredible. I borrowed $15,000 on a line of credit, and turned it into $3 million and over ninety properties in five years.

The twenty-five years of ethical real estate sales experience that followed is now available to you in this book. I hope you learn a few tricks from it.

Not all roads are smooth, but hopefully they lead to the destination you intended. My road had it all.

Hopefully with my assistance, your road will be a straight and profitable one.

CLOSING
THE DEAL

HOW I GOT INTO REAL ESTATE

B ack in 1985, I was a regional manager for Canadian Tire Petroleum Division. My district was the St. Lawrence Division, which was Ottawa to Cornwall to Whitby. Becoming more and more disgruntled about being on the road every day, I listened to some friends who had bought some income properties in the Toronto area. It seemed to be a quicker and easier approach to making my first million.

I bought two houses on my first evening out with my new realtor. I pyramided those properties into ten, and then into forty-eight homes. You can read about this process in my next book.

I am a very trusting person by nature, and was now trusting my agent totally. Big mistake. I purchased a home from him in July 1987 (I think for $351,000 in North York). The appraisal came in at $251,000. His excuses were unbelievable, and I knew by then that I had to get another realtor. Then I thought: Hey, *I* can do this job. And I will do it the only way I know how—honestly.

I always remember how greed ruined a good business relationship. This guy made $600,000 off me alone. And for the sake of one deal, he blew it all. I don't hold a grudge, but I have only spoken to this person once since then. We met at a hockey rink and I took the high road and was very polite. I actually owe him a lot. He gave me great training, great insight and, most importantly, he taught me how much you could lose by being greedy.

Twenty-five years later, I still remember every day. Clients depend on you for the most important purchase of their life, and I appreciate that trust. People who walk in asking about a rental still get the same trust and respect as those clients who have used me for a dozen purchases. My feelings are that we give no one a reason to use anyone else.

My team

I decided to start my team five years ago when I realized that if I was going to continue to grow, I would need help. It turns out that brokerage firms are primarily in the business of recruiting and developing sales professionals, while teams are in the business of generating customers and developing the systems to provide service to them.

Mentoring eleven of the top sales people in the business has turned out to be rewarding and enjoyable. Every day, my agents come to me with questions and situations that are new to them. Most of these adventures I've already experienced, but there is always input from other team members.

We are continuing to grow at a fantastic rate, but are still focused on what got us to where we are today. And that's great customer service. Our phones are always on, and our clients know it. A quick return phone call is always appreciated.

I have implemented business systems that work for each

individual agent. They include Internet, blogging and social networking strategies, lead generations and follow-up systems. We teach each agent how to do successful farming, and how to deal with buyers. They have all been well versed on proper listing presentations.

Each of my agents has set out their real estate business plans, and promotes the team concept of branding and marketing. As in all teams, it's not the name on the back of the jersey—it's the name on the front. The bigger the team becomes, the more leads there will be to go around.

I have built a team that knows achieving real success requires a significant investment of time. Those who achieve outstanding results know that doing so on their own requires them to dedicate the majority of their time to this goal.

My team also knows that I will be investing lots of capital and time in their business. Some portion of their earnings will be dedicated to staff, marketing and building systems.

My wife Janet has been very instrumental in the branding of our team. She has exposed the Al Sinclair Team to more of the GTA and surrounding areas. Some team leaders believe that they have truly built a great team when they are no longer selling or managing. I don't see that day coming for a long time.

Clients: Where do they come from?

Clients, they are everywhere you turn. But once you are known as a salesperson, they don't want you. That's why I have had more success by not pursuing them. In the gym, at the rink, etc., I let them know (over time) what I do. But

I don't EVER solicit. Once I have their trust, and they trust I won't hound them, then I will be answering questions in no time. Be chased, don't be the chaser. It will work, you will see.

Sure, you will answer a lot of favours, but there will be deals in there, and deals pay well. These people also refer you because you are not going to pester their friends. And don't be afraid to give a gift in return for the favour.

When marketing yourself in a paper, magazine, etc., stay the course. Do it for years not weeks or months. People will read your ad or maybe they won't, but they will see it over time and then they will begin to look for it.

I was, and still am, advertising in a small newspaper, the *Beach Metro Community News*. I had been doing an ad for about six months without a single call. Then I went away and didn't do an ad. I got two calls when I got back asking why I hadn't advertised. I guess they thought I went out of business. But that was twenty years ago, and I haven't missed an ad in that paper since. I have sold many houses from that little paper, and received my listings from it as well.

Now with the media changing, we are more active with our website, *The Beach Metro News*, TV ads and TV shows (who'd have thought?). But I still miss those days when I had one ad in the local newspaper and waited for the phone to ring.

Times are a-changing as I see the *Toronto Star* Real Estate section keeps getting smaller and smaller. I spent hundreds of thousands of dollars in that paper, and it seemed to make my clients happy, but didn't sell a lot of homes. Magazines are the same. Remember: don't give anyone a reason to go anywhere else. This is my code. Follow it and you will be successful in real estate.

I was asked to do this book because the publisher bumped into me in a studio and was impressed that our conversation did not revolve around real estate. He said I was pleasant and not intimidating. He then asked me for a card and called me a week later about a property. Oh yeah, always be loaded (with business cards), and when they do call, respond immediately. There is a fine line between a successful and a struggling agent.

Every client does not just represent one deal. They represent a network of friends and family. And each friend and family member represents a new network of friends, and so on... and so on....

Do a good job, stay in touch and use each client as a springboard to a whole new network. I remember in the late '90s I was asked to mentor a new agent. He asked me where to get clients, and he had absolutely no leads. He said to me that the only lead he had was a rental. You know, he did that rental and then started marketing to renters. They all buy in a year or two. In the meantime a thousand bucks here and there ain't shabby.

I remember in the mid '90s when I was with Sutton Group in The Beaches. We had about forty agents, and I was their "numero uno" agent by a long margin. So as I was going past the lobby to get a coffee on a Friday afternoon, I saw a guy in jeans, about thirty-five, at the front desk. Everyone was ignoring this guy like he had the plague. The duty agent didn't come down, and three agents that were there suddenly became too busy. So I asked our secretary if he needed any help. She said that he was looking for a rental in downtown Toronto, and none of the other agents were interested in assisting him. Here I was, the busiest agent in the place, and I'm all over this guy. The other agents thought I was goofy. Well it turns out Brent Graham was Dr. Brent Graham, and his wife was Dr. Helen Macrae. I got them a nice rental for $1,900 a month. They bought a house a year later for over a million bucks. They then started a family, sold their million-dollar home and bought a bigger home. Oh yeah, and they used me in all those listings and sales. You see, I kept in touch, but just as important, I took on the rental. This guy in jeans from Alberta was also the hand doctor for the Toronto Maple Leafs. I love telling this story to anyone who thinks a house or rental is beneath them. I have agents on my team who specialize in rentals. In two or three years those clients will be buying.

Once you have a client's trust, it is so important to keep in touch. I don't like surprises, so I'm not big on phone calls. You don't know what's going on in their life right now, and the call could be very stale. So I follow up with emails, a monthly newsletter that goes to everyone, Christmas cards with a calendar (all personally hand-written), and follow-up letters once a year. Of course, having a lot of "for sale" and "sold" signs doesn't hurt either.

I would say that a key factor to success in real estate sales is consistency. Be reliable, be steady, be consistent. Don't reinvent yourself every couple of years. After awhile, even you won't know who or what you are. My kids call me "Routine Ronny" because I'm a creature of habit. That may not be good for your workouts, but it's great in real estate. Don't change companies all the time, don't go from condos to homes, don't go from specializing in one neighbourhood to another neighbourhood. Be consistent.

Actually, now with the computer age, the city has shrunk to where you can do deals easily, anywhere in the city. Some agents joke that my farm area is Ontario. If I have to drive from Toronto to Oshawa or Burlington a couple of times to do a deal, I'll do it. That truck driver beside you does it every day, and the financial compensation doesn't compare. I actually miss those days because the car is a great place to unwind. Running a team now finds me in the office a lot more and in the car a lot less. But I'm still doing listing appointments and the odd buyer.

Team or individual?

I fought with this decision for years. I actually thought that I could pull this one off myself. Me and an assistant, and low costs! Not a chance, everything became 70 percent me. I had to do it the right way, with the right people. I've played on enough teams to know that it's hard to soar with the eagles when you fly with turkeys.

I guess getting an assistant was my first big step. Boy, did I ever lean on secretaries every day. I know my broker was happy when I hired Jennifer. At first I couldn't keep her busy because I didn't know how to delegate. I did it myself and gave her odd jobs, like faxing and photocopying.

A good assistant wants to be busy and has to be trusted. At first I was wasting time looking for jobs for her to do. Now I think she misses those days. She is swamped and has her own assistant now, who is also swamped. I guess I've learned how to delegate really well.

You owe it to your clients to be the best you can be, to maximize your time and theirs. While I still deal with the odd buyer, I've personally trained my buying agents to be the best, most thorough buying agents anywhere. Bold statement, but not if you can back it up. We do that every day. My buying agents will go anywhere within forty miles of our Beach office. We have certain agents that know the 905 region. We have downtown condo specialists, west end experts and east end experts. Again, some people think my farm area is southern Ontario. Actually, our area of expertise is The Beach and The Bluffs.

My team is trained to know every street thoroughly so that any cold call can be handled quickly and effectively. You only get one chance to make a first impression, and you don't want to waste it. My buyer agents are trained to listen well, ask the proper questions and respond immediately via email with active listings. If there's no email address, then they will fax or hand-deliver them ASAP. "Don't give them a reason to use anyone else,"—that's my slogan. If you follow that, you will do well. When I say well, I mean be in the top 5 percent in the country (that's easy), with an income over $200,000 (no brainer).

When choosing a team, it's not like choosing a sports team where you need to fill all the positions immediately. Real estate is more touchy-feely. You will add team members if you need them and if the right agent is available and eager to work on your team. Remember, these agents are now becoming "dependants," and are relying on your good name. Leads generate a successful career. Add the agents as you need them, but remember that it's your fault as a team leader if you can't keep them busy. You must look at the whole picture, months and years ahead.

What I have done with my team is give them an exciting place to work and a confidence that they are on the top team in Toronto, and one of the top teams in North America. I get calls every week about our reputation as a team, and individuals want to join us. I have never solicited an agent (except my wife), but now have eleven agents, two assistants, a stager and a photographer on our roster. One thing that I demand is that they treat this opportunity as a career. Pay cheques are not bonuses, they are your salary. Over the years, after I've finished a deal with an agent, some can't wait to tell me how they are now going away for three weeks on a holiday. Now there goes their money and their momentum. In hockey, one of my coaches told me that we had an extra player on the ice called "Mo"(mentum). It's such an important ingredient, and once you get it, try not to let it go. Of course, you have to get away now and then or you'll go nuts. From May 2001 to the World Cup of Oldertimers' hockey in 2007, I didn't take a vacation. Some guy I am, my first vacation in six years and I take my wife Janet to Sweden so she can watch me play hockey. I made it up to her on the way back by taking her to London and Paris. She'd never been to Europe before so it was a blast. Oh yeah, and we won the gold over there (beat the Swedes 5-2 in the final).

I remember one vacation in 1998. We had a 42-foot Sea Ray, and took the kids to Alexandria Bay across Lake Ontario for one week. It went from costing me about $2,000, to costing me $10,000. While away, a client bought a home for $400,000 in The Beaches area, on Leuty Avenue. Why do I remember the street? Because it cost me $10,000. After that, I swore, no more vacations. But you know, it was my fault, I should have had someone with the client during that time. They didn't have buyer broker contracts back then. If they did, I would have had her sign it.

Buyer broker contracts—boy did I fight that one. I just could not understand how it benefited the buyer. To be honest, I still don't, but I get my agents to have all their clients sign them. You can't believe how bad it feels when a client who you think is yours suddenly pulls out a contract. Poof... there goes 2.5 percent!

As a buyer, make sure you are 100 percent sure that this is the agent you want to work with. If not, just sign it for that one deal (which could be seven days for that property address). I'm fighting with an agent right now who came out of the woodwork. A buyer with one of my listings bought from me. He wasn't sure what he had signed with his other agent, but was pretty sure it wasn't a buyer broker. So he called the guy, who blew him off and then called him back five days later saying: "Sorry, I was under the weather". Well, I reduced my commission by a point because I did both ends. Then this guy surfaces again saying he has a buyer broker. You think he would have remembered that when the buyer called him. To say the least, this buyer broker has caused a lot of difficult situations, but I love a good fight, especially when I'm right. Oh yeah, I have everything signed. Remember, always have paperwork. In this business, it is so important.

Realtors get a bad rap sometimes. We are compared to car salesmen, lawyers, and so on. But I would say that 75 percent are pretty good. Wow, that leaves a quarter of them out there as someone I would keep an eye on.

My theory is that agents get in the real estate business with good intentions. They're basically good people who want to make a good (great) living and still keep their integrity. But something happens, and they change. Maybe it's the money, maybe it's the fame (yeah right!), but fortunately it is only a quarter of them. But like any profession, there is a high turnover. Ryan Taylor, on my team, figures that he is the only one left in the business from his class of 2008. That is a remarkable statistic.

This is why teams are so good for agents just starting out. They get well qualified leads in a steady manner. They get all their expenses (except cell phone and gas) paid for. This includes any marketing and advertising materials they may need. Other costs that I pay for include all licencing fees (RECO, TREB, OREA, and CREA). I also cover all company costs. These costs all add up, and are all on my dime. Now that I see all that I'm giving away, I feel a bit like Santa Claus. Actually, it's a win-win situation for everybody.

I run a no-nonsense team, but we have a good time. As long as my agents are working hard, they'll be producing. I demand that they open house every weekend and check in on weekdays. I talk to each of them almost every day; but my big contribution is twenty-five years of experience. They ask for a lot of advice, and I enjoy giving it to them. We have team meetings every two weeks or so.

Now that the team has been running for almost five

years, they are all becoming a lot more independent. Pretty soon, I'll be coming to them with questions. I want them all to grow as professionals because the stronger they become, the stronger the team becomes. Once my agents are licenced, it's important to keep that licence. In twenty-five years of selling, I have never had an ethics charge or been reported to RECO (Real Estate Council of Ontario).

About eight years ago, a fellow agent was reported to RECO (the watchdog that monitors, fines and suspends agents for violations). He was so nervous that he could lose his licence. He said to me, "Al, I can't lose my ticket because I couldn't make this kind of money without breaking the law." I remember two things about that: one, his nervous temper and anxiety; and two, those words.

It is the temptation of commissions and deals that make good people do bad things or cut corners. Cutting corners is the most frequent mistake made by realtors.

Am I ready to buy, or should I wait?

Is the market going to stay strong? Or should I wait until it weakens? These are the questions that every first-time home buyer and general buyer asks themselves. You will get dozens of different opinions at every party you attend, but remember, skeptics are generally looking for ways to knock the housing market down a peg or two. In general, it is better to buy at today's prices. Over the last twenty-five years, only during 1989 and for a short period in 2008 and early 2009, did prices fall. Records indicate that playing the waiting game is usually an expensive gamble. Follow the interest rates, and if the five-year rate is still traditionally low, then the market will normally be healthy. Remember, renting is just making someone else richer. Home ownership is forced savings. Every time you make a mortgage payment, you pay down the principle. Besides, we all need a place to live. I'll tell you, rental properties do not come close to homes you buy to live in. So keep an eye on the interest rate changes when deciding on when to buy. Some of the factors that will affect interest rates are Canadian growth rate numbers. Low rates limit the downside of any extended weakness. Another factor is healthy employment. Always watch out for the employment figures as that positive outlook will bode well for a steady growth in the housing market. Healthy market conditions will always support growth in the average selling price. But there will always be skeptics because even with low interest rates, analysts and households will analyze their debt acquired in the good times, and delay, possibly missing a lower market. It's better to buy at today's prices.

The media and some analysts will always lead us to believe that the Canadian housing market is a bubble ready to burst.

I have friends who got into some pretty cool digs back in the '80s. The rent was low, and it was just too good to be true. The fact is that some are now in their fifties and are still renting the same place. They can't afford to get into the Toronto real estate market, and they will continue to rent forever. They have no equity, which is our best and most consistent method of forced savings.

Interest rates are not supposed to increase much in the next few years (as of 2011), so we expect this current market to continue strongly. Periods of severe price declines were characterized by double-digit interest rates and high un-employment rates. Today we have low unemployment rates and fifty-year low interest rates.

Another strong factor in the Canadian housing market is our very strict Canadian banking system. The Canadian housing market is unlikely to suffer a U.S.-style collapse ever, of any magnitude. This is a key and overriding difference in the quality of the loan origination in the past decade, as well as other institutional factors, such as mortgage insurance and recourse against faulters. Canada has not experienced widespread speculations and ridiculously loose credit standards. Instead, Canada's housing market will remain reasonably affordable because of its low interest rates.

What got the Americans in such a mess was them assuming that their economy would continue to rise at record numbers. I remember reading a very respectable American house magazine (I used to read *Sports Illustrated*, and now I read a lot of house and décor magazines. Ah, getting old is fun!). Anyways, this magazine read: "Location, design and quality matter... so does the financing". IMAGINE a million-dollar loan payment with payments of only $2,396 per month, and with 100 percent financing:

- No down payment.
- Interest-only payments.
- No qualification.

Wow... sign me up. And they did. But this caused widespread speculation, and what goes up (that fast) must come down. And it did. The Canadian banking system would never allow this to happen, so rest assured that we will not see this happen in Canada. In the States, there are foreclosures everywhere, and hardly any construction at any housing developments, even at such low prices.

Another factor in Canada, especially in the southern Ontario market, is the rising population. There are so many immigrants always looking for housing. If they buy the starter homes, they will bump up those homeowners to a higher priced market, and so on.

Toronto, for instance, is considered one of the most important North American gateways, described by some as a world-class city with great potential for investments. It's been designated as Canada's top market, with Vancouver being the only competitive rival. A considerable portion of Toronto's market success is owed to the magnitude of private investors and immigrants who are constantly investing in our market—especially the high-rise condo market. Approximately 80,000 new immigrants settle in the Greater Toronto Area (GTA) each year. They fill up our condo buildings, our rental apartments and multi-unit investment properties.

However, this construction will not be able to house the 80,000 new immigrants. Construction must continue and must pick up. I remember driving along the Gardiner Expressway and wondering how these places would ever be filled. Well, twenty years later, we need more cranes in the air. We need more homes in the 905 region, and we need more projects in the core of Toronto.

It is widely understood that mortgage interest rates are not going to rise sharply, and any sense of a slight recession will not happen until the end of the decade, at the earliest. Affordability is the best it's been in a long time when you consider the average income for a standard home. A five-year fixed mortgage and a 25-year amortization will cost less than the recommended affordability rate of 32 percent of your income.

BUYERS GUIDE

Since buying a home is probably the largest, most important and most expensive purchase you will ever make, I will try and make the process as smooth as I can.

Affordability

Since there is such a variety of shapes, sizes and costs—knowing what you can afford at the beginning of your search saves you time and frustration later on.

I have had clients call me and say that they want to start looking. I ask where, and they say they "are not too picky". I say, "Okay, what style?" and they reply, "Oh, I'm pretty easy". I ask, "Okay then, how much?" and they respond that they're not sure. Well that limits my search to about 40,000 homes. So let's qualify the buyer.

RULE A

Banks and trust companies allow you to spend approximately 32 percent of your gross monthly income on housing costs (including property taxes, heating, and if applicable, 50 percent of the condominium fees). The ratio of debt to income is referred to as the gross debt service, or GDS.

The following calculation will show you how much you can afford monthly for housing.

Your gross monthly income _____

Spouses gross monthly income _____

Other gross monthly income _____

Total monthly income _____

Monthly income × 32% = GDS

RULE B

The second affordability rule is that your entire monthly debt load should not be more than 40 percent of your gross monthly income. This includes housing costs and other debts, such as car loans and credit card payments. Lenders add up these debts to determine what percentage they are of your gross household monthly income. This is your total debt service (TDS) ratio.

The following calculation will show you what you can afford for housing, including your outstanding debts.

A) Monthly income from your GDS calculations above × 40% = TDS _____

B) Add up your monthly payments for loans, credit cards and other debts _____

Monthly income left for housing costs (subtract the amount of A from the amount of B).

In addition to GDS and TDS ratios, financial institutions base their lending decision on your credit history, job stability, and the amount of your down payment. Interest rates also affect the amount of financing you will be able to obtain. Remember that many lenders are willing to exceed these guidelines.

EXAMPLE

Bob earns $40,000 annually, and his wife Jill earns $43,000. They have monthly car payments of $350, and a credit card payment of $150 per month.

<u>How much can they afford for housing?</u>
Bob's monthly income ($40,000 / 12) = $3,333
Jill's monthly income ($43,500 / 12) = $3,625
Total   = $6,958
GDS ($6,958 × 32%)   = $2,226.56
<u>Monthly debts</u>
Car payment $350
Credit card payment $150
Monthly housing cost $2,226.56
Total = $2,726.56
TDS ($2,726.56 / $6,958) = 39%

Because their total debt including housing costs and all other monthly debts does not exceed 40%, they can afford to purchase a home.

FINANCING

Pre-Approval

It is important to be qualified or pre-approved for financing before you start looking for a home. This lets you and your realtor know what you can afford as well as providing a written confirmation or certificate for a fixed interest rate good for a specific period of time. To obtain pre-approval, contact your realtor or mortgage broker. The benefit of a mortgage broker is that they operate independently of the lender and therefore can assist you in finding the best financial product at the best rate from a variety of sources; and usually at no expense to you.

Conventional mortgages

The maximum amount of a conventional mortgage is 80 percent of the purchase price. The amortization period to repay the loan is usually twenty-five years. The term of the mortgage is the number of months or years, usually six months to five years, for which the rate of interest is set.

High ratio mortgages

For most people, the hardest part of buying a home—especially the first one—is saving the necessary down payment. With mortgage loan insurance, you can put as little as 5 percent down. Mortgage loan insurance protects the lender and, by law, most Canadian lending institutions require it. The cost of high ratio mortgage loan insurance is in the form of a premium. The premium is calculated as a percentage of the principle and can be paid in a single lump sum or be added to your mortgage and included in your monthly payments.

Down payment	Loan insurance
5% to 9.9%	2.75%
10% to 14.9%	2%
15% to 19.9%	1.75%

HIGH RATIO MORTGAGE EXAMPLE

Purchase price	$350,000
5% down payment	$ 17,500
Mortgage required	$332,500
Insurance premium	$ 9,143.75($332,500 × 2.75%)
Total mortgage amount	$341,643.75 ($332,500 / $9,143.75)

The 5 percent down payment

The down payment is usually derived from a buyer's accumulated savings or a gift from an immediate relative. The buyer may also be eligible to either receive a "cash back" from the lender, which can be used as the down payment; or to borrow the required funds.

Using your RRSP to purchase a home

This program allows each RRSP plan holder to borrow up to $25,000 from the plan to use toward the down payment of a home. Couples with separate plans can borrow up to $25,000 each to a total of $50,000. Home buyers using this program have up to fifteen years to return the monies, interest free, to their RRSP. Using these funds towards the purchase of a home does not deregister the plan unless the monies are not returned as agreed, thereby allowing participants to retain the tax advantages the RRSP offers.

Here are the major guidelines for this program:

- You are a first-time buyer or have not owned a principal residence in Canada during the past four years;
- The RRSP must have been in existence for at least 90 days;
- You must be a resident of Canada both at the time the funds are withdrawn and at the time the home is acquired;
- A minimum of 1/15 of the amount withdrawn has to be repaid annually;
- Repayment of more than 1/15 of the borrowed amount in any particular year will be carried forward and can be applied towards a future year's repayment.

Not every RRSP is eligible under this program. Check with your investment firm to see if you qualify. Also, advise your lawyer well before closing that you will be using these funds.

Additional Costs of Buying

Home inspection

A home inspection is strongly recommended for most residential properties, and will usually be a condition of the offer. Your sales representative can assist you in choosing a home inspector. The cost will vary depending on the value, age and use of the property, but will usually range from $350 to $500.

Termite inspection

You may wish to hire a termite inspector as well as a home inspector if you are buying in an area of the city where termites are known to be a problem. This could add another $200 to $300 to the cost of your inspection.

Appraisal fees

When you apply for a mortgage, the lender will want to see an appraisal on the property to ensure that the price you are paying falls within the accepted range of value for that type of property and that area of the city. The fee for this is usually between $250 and $350.

Land survey

When you make an offer on a freehold property, you will usually ask the seller to provide a copy of the survey for the property. The purpose of this survey is to show the boundaries as well as the footprint of the building on the site. If there is no survey available, you may wish to hire a surveyor to prepare one at a cost of approximately $1,000 to $2,000.

Title insurance

Title insurance provides insurance against the future costs of remedying most problems with the title on your property. Ask your sales representative to explain the benefits and the cost of this service.

Land transfer tax

The tax rates on the value of the consideration are:

Percentage	Explanation
0.5%	Amounts up to and including $55,000

Percentage	Explanation
1.0%	Amounts exceeding $55,000 up to and including $250,000
1.5%	Amounts exceeding $250,000
2.0%	Amounts exceeding $400,00 where the land contains one or two single family residences

Applicable taxes

The seller is required to pay the HST on the real estate commission. Buyers are responsible for paying applicable taxes on appraisal services, land survey, home inspection, termite inspection, lawyer's fees, and on the premium charged on CMHC loans or Genworth Financial Canada.

HST

The HST tax payable usually comes as a surprise to most sellers. It is a fee that is collected by the realtor and must be paid to the Government. Therefore, it is very important that the agents pay this HST every quarter. Because it is 13 percent on top of commissions, agents suddenly find that they have this huge HST bill. Remember, it's not your money, it's the Government's—and sellers must pay it.

Offers

When your agent is preparing an offer, make it a clean offer. A clean offer is one that isn't full of clauses that will concern the seller. Some clauses are impossible to meet, and since you have the buyer's hopes up, the deal has no chance.

Standard conditions, such as financing and home inspection are okay, so is insurance; but sometimes having conditions on the sale of another property may be pushing it.

If I am representing the vendor, I will always make sure that the other property is well priced and well marketed because now you are basically waiting for two houses to sell.

LET'S MAKE AN OFFER

You've found that perfect house—what do you do now? Your sales representative will prepare an agreement of purchase and sale, including any custom clauses you may require. Most buyers will make an offer provided certain conditions are met. They may include:

Financing approved

Even if you have been pre-approved for a mortgage, the property will require an appraisal to assure the lender that the price you are paying falls within accepted market value. Once your financing has been approved, you are required to provide written notice to the seller in the form of a waiver of amendment before the expiry of the condition.

FINTRAC (The Financial Transactions and Reports Analysis Centre of Canada)

As of June 23, 2008, for every purchase and sale in real estate, the brokerage must obtain an Individual Client Information Record. This record sets out the buyer's/

seller's name and address, and the nature of your principal business/occupation, and date of birth. You will need to show a piece of identification that confirms your identity, for example: birth certificate, driver's licence, passport.

Elements of the Offer:

Irrevocable date

For the offer to be valid, it must contain a number of specific dates and times. Your initial offer will be valid for a specific period of time, usually until midnight of the same day or the following day, after which the offer is deemed to be dead. This timeframe is called the irrevocable period.

Do not make this date more than 24 hours (usually it's 10 p.m. that evening) because it gives the others a chance to bid against you.

Completion date

This is the date set for the transfer of ownership of the property negotiated between you and the seller, and can also be referred to as the closing date. Closing dates are generally thirty, sixty or ninety days.

Requisition date

This is the period in which your lawyer must determine if there are any problems with the title of the property, and is usually set thirty days prior to the completion date.

The deposit

A deposit cheque must accompany the offer to the seller. The amount of the deposit will vary depending upon the value of the property, but usually represents between 5 percent and 10 percent of the purchase price.

Fixtures

Fixtures are any items permanently attached to the property. For example, a bathtub, sink or toilet permanently plumbed in would be a fixture. Technically, anything nailed to the building is a fixture, while items screwed on (because screws can be removed) are chattels. This is often an area of contention when buying a resale home. So be aware of this distinction and, if in doubt, put it in the offer.

Chattels

Chattels, unlike fixtures, are not deemed to be part of the property, and must be specified in the offer if you want them included in the sale. The following are some items you may wish to include in the offer: area rugs, ceiling fans, chandeliers and other light fixtures, draperies, wood burning stoves and accessories, microwave ovens, refrigerators/ freezers, stoves and ovens, washers and dryers, window air conditioners, garage door openers, storage sheds, swing sets and other playground equipment, garden furniture, barbecues, central vacuums and equipment.

As an agent I try not to get too hung up on chattels. I tell people that we are selling a home, so let's focus. I have seen many agents blow a great deal for their buyer because they couldn't get a washing machine. That's madness! However, as a seller I tell my vendor that the buyers have put together all of their money for the deposit and down payment, and there isn't anything left for appliances. So instead of having them walk, let's consider including the fridge and stove.

Negotiating the offer

After signing the offer, your sales representative will register it with the listing brokerage. A time will be set for the listing sales representative and your sales representative to meet and present the offer to the seller. The seller has a number of options available:

- Reject the offer;
- Accept the offer exactly as presented, making no changes;
- Make a counter-offer back to you with whatever changes the seller wants, such as price, closing or conditions. You then have the option of accepting the seller's counter-offer or of making your own changes and signing the newly-amended offer back to them. This is where your sales representative's negotiation skills come into play.

I love this part of my job. I guess it's the hockey player in me, but I love to win. And I want to win all offer negotiations. I have heard agents tell me that it's the worst part of selling real estate, that their stomachs get tied in knots. It's like football: you practice all week for Sunday games. Offers are simply "gametime". May the best negotiator win.

BUYING A CONDO

Condominiums have grown in popularity over the past three decades as an alternative form of home ownership. If you are considering this option, the following information should prove helpful.

A condominium can be an ideal starter home since it may cost considerably less than single family homes in the same neighbourhood. However, a condominium can restrict your freedom through a list of rules and bylaws governing how you may use the unit. It's important to be fully aware of the corporation's bylaws before you buy.

How do co-ops and co-ownerships differ from condominiums?

In equity co-operative, the owner is not registered on title but receives a form of proprietary ownership. The corporation is registered on title and issues a share certificate to each owner. The corporation owns the property, and the rights of occupation come from a separate agreement that sets out the exclusive right of each owner to occupy a certain unit. This agreement also sets out the owner's obligations to pay a proportionate share of the building's mortgage, operating expenses and property taxes. Since responsibility for payment of taxes and mortgage in a co-op is joint, if one owner goes into default, the other owners must make up the shortfall or risk losing their equity. Many older co-ops have no mortgage, and buyers must pay cash since most banks are reluctant to finance share certificates. However, there are some institutions that provide financing for these types of properties.

In a co-ownership, each buyer has their percentage interest in the property registered on title. Possession of an individual unit in the property comes by way of a separate agreement which sets out each owner's rights and responsibilities. Mortgages are often available for this type of property through credit unions and trust companies. Have your sales representative check with the listing sales representative.

Condo sales are at an all-time high. In cities like Toronto and Vancouver, people are rediscovering the joys of living downtown again, along with the low maintenance and easy lifestyle that goes with having your very own castle in the clouds. And with housing real estate prices at truly stratospheric levels across the country, a condo is an affordable way into the market, especially for young people.

Buying and selling real estate has become very specialized the last few years. So when looking for a lawyer/notary, make sure it's a real estate lawyer/notary: one who spends most of their time closing real estate deals.

And don't wait until after the deal is struck before choosing a lawyer; then you lose the valuable input they can provide by scrutinizing the offer before your pen hits the paper. Since your lawyer's role is part advisor, part confidant and part nursemaid, a good rapport with your lawyer is a must.

How can you find a good real estate lawyer? Ask friends, family, neighbours and co-workers who they've used in the past; and get several names from your realtor or banker too.

Never choose a real estate lawyer/notary just because their fees are the lowest. As with any other professional, quality and experience is the key, not just price.

How are condominiums owned?

Condominium ownership is generally divided between two or more parties, each of whom owns a portion of the structure separately and a portion of it in common. For instance, if you are an owner in a high-rise apartment building where there are several other owners, you own a unit individually, and it is legally registered in your name. You also own a proportionate share of the common areas in the development. These generally include the outside grounds, recreational facilities, lobby, stairs, halls and elevators, as well as the air conditioning, electrical and plumbing systems. Some common areas may be reserved for the exclusive use of specific owners, such as roof gardens, balconies, parking spaces and storage lockers.

As a unit owner, you are automatically a member of the condominium corporation. In essence, you're a voting member of a self-governing community with one vote per unit.

What is included in the maintenance fees?

In addition to the costs associated with owning your own unit (mortgage payments, taxes, and so on), you are also required to pay your share of the cost of maintaining the common areas in the monthly maintenance fee. It's important to know what is and is not included in your maintenance fee. For example, heat may be included while the cost of electricity may not be.

What is a reserve fund?

In Ontario, at least 10 percent of this maintenance fee must be held in a reserve fund to pay for major repairs on items like heating systems, roofs and plumbing. If you are considering buying a unit in an older building, be sure that the reserve fund is sufficient to pay for any anticipated major repairs. Newer buildings may not have had time to accumulate a large reserve fund. Information on the status of the building's reserve fund is contained in the Status Certificate.

How does the Condominium Act affect me?

As of May 5, 2001, an updated set of rules now govern all Ontario condominiums under the Condominium Act of 1998. The following are some features of the Act, which took effect in July, 2001.

All condominium corporations must conduct a periodic reserve fund study to make sure the fund is adequate to deal with future needs.

A Status Certificate replaces the former Estoppel Certificate. It provides a wide range of information on the building, including: common expenses, status of the reserve fund as well as any plans to increase the reserve fund, a copy of the current declaration, bylaws and rules, a copy of the current budget, a list of agreements with the corporation, information about the most recent reserve fund study, and information about insurance policies. The maximum charge for this certificate is $100, and is best reviewed by your lawyer.

Condominium status certificate

This condition applies only to the purchase of the condominium. It allows your solicitor to review the condominium's documents to ensure the corporation is financially sound and meets all the requirements of the Condominium Act. Under the new Condominium Act, the property management company has up to ten days to prepare the Status Certificate, and can charge a maximum of $100 for the service.

Completing the Sale

The role of your lawyer

Your lawyer's job is to certify good and marketable title to the property, free of encumbrances, liens and judgments. Your sales representative will deliver all documentation to your lawyer related to the sale.

Registering the mortgage

The lawyer receives instructions from the mortgage company, prepares the draft mortgage document, forwards the draft to the lender, makes amendments if required, and arranges for you to sign the documents. The mortgage company then releases the funds to your lawyer. Some lenders prefer to pay the property taxes on your behalf to ensure that the taxes are never in arrears. In this case, the mortgagee will hold back a certain amount from the advance on closing to start a tax account. Your payment will include the taxes in addition to the regular principal and interest. Check with your mortgage representative to see how your taxes will be handled.

Insurance

You are required to place fire insurance on the property. The coverage should be for at least the amount of the mortgage to be acceptable to the mortgage company. A guaranteed replacement clause is usually acceptable, and must take effect on the closing date.

Statement of adjustments

The closing balance to be paid by the buyer is "subject to the usual adjustments." The statement of adjustments is a system of credits and debits whereby amounts are added to or subtracted from the balance to be paid by the buyer, depending on whether or not the seller has paid certain items in advance. The day of closing is assigned to the buyer, who is responsible for taxes and utilities from 12:01 a.m. of that day. For example, taxes might have been paid up to date after the scheduled closing, so the buyer will credit the seller for the exact number of days "overpaid". The same applies to water rates and fuel. Utility companies are notified of the change of ownership by your lawyer, and final meter readings are arranged for the date of closing.

Legal fees

A lawyer will usually charge between $750 and $1,000, plus disbursements, for a straightforward real estate transaction. This is payable prior to closing.

Land transfer tax

Payable by the buyer on closing. The tax is based on the purchase price.

Provincial Land Transfer Tax formula:

0.5% on the first $55,000, *plus*:
1% of the amount from $55,001 to $250,000
1.5% of the amount in excess of $250,001 to $400,000
2% of the amount in excess of $400,000

As of February 1st, 2008, any properties purchased in the Metro Toronto Area are subject to a Municipal Land Transfer tax, which will be levied on top of the Provincial Land Transfer Tax.

Day of closing

The lawyers or clerks exchange documents and funds to close the transaction. You can expect to get access to your new home by late afternoon on that day, but check with your lawyer. Changing locks is recommended after closing as a safety precaution. If you have any dead-bolt locks on your doors, it is a simple matter to remove the cylinder and replace it with a new one.

I have agents tell me that they leave town the day they have a closing. I have never heard of anything so irresponsible in my life. They don't want the last-minute problem phone calls, I guess. I make sure we are there for every closing, and will guide the buyer and seller through the process (with 290 sales in 2010, I sure would have been away a lot of days). I am certain those agents that I'm talking about don't have many repeat buyers or sellers.

Home operating costs

The following is an estimate of the costs involved in the normal operation of a home in the Toronto area. Costs vary from one area of the city to another, so these figures should be used only as a guide.

Realty taxes

Property owners have the option of paying their property taxes in eight installments over the course of the calendar year. Mortgage companies may insist that they pay the property tax and collect it with your monthly mortgage payment. Realty taxes range from $1,000 to $5,000 a year and up depending on the size and location of the property. Taxes are reassessed on an ongoing basis.

Heating

Home heating will usually be provided by natural gas, oil or electricity. Costs vary depending on the type of fuel, size of home, amount of insulation, exposure and usage.

Electricity

Costs vary greatly depending on usage, e.g. how many people you have in the home, the size of your home, how many energy efficient cost measures you have undertaken (such as energy saver appliances). Usually billing is every second month, or you can go on equal billing and pay monthly.

Insurance

Insurance is essential for all homeowners, and is required by your mortgage company before it will release the funds to close the deal. Premiums are based on the replacement cost of the building, and start at around $350 to $700 per year.

Water and solid waste management

Most properties in Toronto are now on water meters, and are billed according to usage. As of November 1st, 2008, your water bill will also include a fee for solid waste management. Your solid waste management fee will pay for garbage, recycling, green bin, litter prevention, landfill management, and other diversion programs. These utility bills will be sent about three times a year.

The following list indicates some of the things to do in preparation for your move:

- Notify the post office, and send out change of address cards.
- Notify your insurance company that you have purchased, and you require fire insurance coverage as of the date of closing. Provide them with the name, address and telephone number of your lawyer so that a "binder" for the coverage on your new home and contents will be forwarded to your lawyer at least one week in advance of closing.
- Notify the Ministry of Transportation that you are moving, and have your driver's licence amended to show the new address.
- Notify the utility companies of your change of address. Your lawyer may do this. Final meter readings are necessary for transferring of accounts. Here are some useful phone numbers.

Toronto Hydro
(416) 542-8000

Enbridge Gas
(416) 492-5100

- Arrange for new telephone service and installation of jacks if required.
- Arrange for cable television hook-up.
- Notify all newspaper and other publication subscriptions of change of address.
- Notify your bank of your change of address, and order new personalized cheques.

FREQUENTLY ASKED QUESTIONS: BUYERS

Many buyers do not fully understand the home buying process and what role a real estate sales representative plays. The following are some of the most frequently asked questions that buyers ask or don't fully understand.

What does it cost as a buyer to use a sales representative?

The compensation that a sales representative receives typically comes from the seller's proceeds. In other words, there is no cost for a buyer to use a sales representative in a traditional sales representative/buyer relationship. In a buyer agency agreement, there may be some cost to the buyer, but even their agreements are usually worded so that the sales representative is compensated from the seller.

Can my sales representative give me information regarding properties from other companies?

Yes, if that other company is a member of Multiple Listing Services (MLS), which most real estate companies are. For Sale By Owner (FSBO) properties are not listed in MLS, so a sales representative likely would not be able to provide information regarding them. However, with a Buyer Representation Agreement, your sales representative may be able to help you purchase a FBSO.

What if I find a property on my own?

You should contact your sales representative and not the property owner or the sales representative listing the property. Having the address or the MLS number is very helpful and will assist your sales representative in gathering information regarding the property.

What type of information will my sales representative need from me?

A sales representative will need any type of information regarding the property you are looking for that is important to you. For example, the number of bedrooms, garage size, price, location and number of bathrooms are common criteria. Other considerations include the school district, type of home (ranch, tri-level, etc.), and room sizes. Keep in mind that a search that is too specific may narrow your list of properties too much, while one that is too broad may give you more properties to look at than you have time to go through.

Can I go to open houses without my sales representative?

You can go to open houses without your sales representative. However, you must inform the attending sales representative that you already have your own sales representative working for you.

How can I find out about new properties?

Your sales representative should be able to accommodate your particular situation whether it is via email, phone calls, etc. Clients with email capability can receive automatic updates from the MLS system as soon as new listings are entered.

What if I am unhappy and want to switch sales representatives?

Let the first sales representative know that you are unhappy and the reason why. See if you can work out the issues with them.

Summary

When purchasing real estate, a sales representative can be an invaluable resource if you remember your responsibilities:

1. Work with just one sales representative.
2. Make sure you tell your sales representative everything.
3. Always tell other sales representatives you are already working with a sales representative.
4. Have a buyer representation agreement signed.

And remember: do the honourable thing. If you have signed a buyers agreement, tell the selling agent right from the start. Too many times we have worked with clients for weeks, even after asking them, and then out of the woodwork comes an agent, usually looking for a free paycheque. Well it becomes a real mess. So be upfront and everyone is satisfied. Too many times, salespeople are deemed to be dishonest or less than honourable. But you know, there usually are two sides to every story.

BEFORE YOU START

1. Hire a professional realtor to help with the buying process. It costs you nothing since the seller pays the commission.

   And remember, every call a realtor gets is a privilege. Make sure they give you every attention to detail, return calls promptly, and are good negotiators. I have actually had agents tell me that the worst part of being a realtor was the negotiating. I say, "That's when the fun begins". I have been in numerous transactions where I felt sorry for the agent's clients. They had poor representation, and I was winning… big time.

   And make sure that if anybody is referred to you, they give you three choices. Don't be fooled by a lawyer's office. Expensive high-rise buildings do not make a realtor any better, usually just more expensive.

2. Make sure you have a good lawyer. When shopping around for one, a client will usually get a quotation for the lawyer's fees plus disbursements and taxes. Disbursements typically include title insurance, title search costs, land registration charges, conveyance software charges, office expenses (such as photocopying, couriers, etc.), off-title inquires, and sometimes a property tax certificate. These are hard costs that the lawyer will incur and pass along to the client. Sometimes

clients will ask for a flat fee quotation inclusive of fees and disbursements. However, a lawyer who does their job properly understands that it is difficult to provide such a figure because at the time a quote is given, not everything about the property will be known. There may be other instruments clouding title which need to be examined and dealt with accordingly.

A simple condo purchase will most likely have separate property identification numbers, and therefore, separate parcel registration showing the history of title for each condo dwelling unit, the condo parking unit, and the condo locker unit. During the course of a real estate transaction, it is impossible to predict all the variables and contingencies that may influence the quality of the ownership a purchaser seeks to obtain when buying a home. It is up to the lawyer to make sure a purchaser gets marketable title, and that a seller complies with the requisitions to provide same.

Some lawyers' websites will have an all inclusive fee calculator that will purportedly give the client an all inclusive cost for service. Most of these fee calculators are illusionary and confusing, showing you bolded numbers as your bottom line, and random small numbers that somehow you end up paying but were not part of the bolded bottom line figure.

3. Seek financial qualification to determine how much mortgage you can afford.

Mortgage Qualifying

Do you know whether you qualify for a mortgage and, if you do, do you know how much you can afford? Before you can even begin to think about buying a home, you should answer both of these crucial questions.

Qualifying for a mortgage

Most lenders look at five factors when determining whether you qualify for a mortgage loan:

1. Income.
2. Debts.
3. Employment history.
4. Credit history.
5. Value of the property you want to buy.

One of the first questions a lender will consider is how much of your total income you'll be spending on housing. This helps the lender decide whether you can comfortably afford a house.

A lender will then look at your debts, which generally include house payments as well as payments on all loans, charge cards, child support, etc., that you make each month.

A history of steady employment, usually within the same job for several years, helps you to qualify. But a short history in your current job shouldn't prevent you from getting a loan as long as there have been no gaps in income over the last two years.

Good credit is very important in qualifying for a loan,

and the lender will want to know what the house is worth and the price you plan to pay.

How much can you afford?

The size of your down payment affects the amount of your monthly mortgage payments. A smaller down payment will mean your monthly mortgage payments will be higher, but it may allow you to buy sooner rather than later.

A down payment of 25 percent or more will qualify you for a conventional mortgage. If it is less than 25 percent, the mortgage must be insured with a mortgage insurance company, such as Genworth Financial Canada. Homes can be purchased with as little as 5 percent down.

Mortgage payments for principal, interest and taxes generally should not exceed 30 percent of your gross monthly income. Simply multiply your gross monthly income by 0.03 to determine your maximum monthly payments. If your gross monthly income is $4,000, the most you can afford is $4,000 × 0.03 = $1,200.

Don't forget closing costs such as land transfer tax, legal fees, building inspection, home insurance and realtor fees, which can amount to 1.5 percent of the purchase price.

When budgeting, also consider other monthly-related expenses such as condominium fees, heat, hydro, water, property tax, insurance and household maintenance.

And one last tip: get a pre-approved mortgage. This free service from lenders comes with no obligations, helps to confirm your financial boundaries, and frees you to focus on finding the home you want.

Location

There is a saying about opening a restaurant: "The three important things are LOCATION, LOCATION, LOCATION". Buying a home, while it is not a restaurant, also requires this simple piece of wisdom. Choosing a proper location is the single most important consideration to buying a new home. While part of the new home can be repaired, replaced, or even an entire house can be rebuilt—you are stuck with the location of your new home. The choice you make for the location of your new home will stay with you for the rest of your life (or at least until you move). A bad choice in location will haunt you till the end of your days (or until moving day if you move again).

While every individual or family has their own require-ments of convenience and preference for location, here are some factors to watch out for when choosing a location for buying your new home. Convenience for travel to work and/or school is the first thing to look for. Unless you are retired (or a lottery winner), chances are you will spend half your waking life at work or school. If you drive to work, is the location of your new home close enough to your place of work or school?

There are some people who drive more than two hundred miles to get to work every day! While this sounds like it borders on insanity, they probably made a poor choice in selecting a location for their new home. In bad weather or emergency situations, it is better to be able to return home quickly without trekking through half the province. If you commute, look for convenient commuting options such as buses, trains, or even car pools. While you can drive and park at a train station, for example, it should not be so far away as to take up half your day just to commute to work from your new home.

Another factor to consider in the convenience corner is the closeness of other members of your family (or good friends). In the unfortunate event of a personal emergency, can a family member or friend reach your home promptly? Being all alone in a new neighbourhood can also make for lonely times if you are so far away that other family members cannot visit you easily, and vice versa, where you would not be able to visit them easily either. Accessibility to shopping and groceries is another important factor to keep in mind. While you do not want to live next to a supermarket for obvious traffic reasons, is it close enough so you can drive there quickly in an emergency (storms, blizzards, etc.)? If you have kids then there will likely be a milk run every day or every few days, so short of keeping a cow in a garage, is there more than one grocery store within easy reach should you run out of food or milk, which can happen in times of emergencies?

If you have children, proximity to parks or similar recreation facilities is very important. You really can't expect to drive a four-year-old twenty miles to play in a park. Children make friends in such social meeting places, and having friends to play with is a critical element in any child's development. Emergency services are another thing to look at. Is there a firehouse close enough to your new home location? Is there a hospital or medical facility near enough to reach quickly in the event of a health emergency? Is there a police station or sheriff/law enforcement presence nearby where they can respond quickly to assist you if need be? Crime can happen anywhere, and having a police or law enforcement presence nearby will keep your mind at ease.

You also have to make sure that your new home is in a safe neighbourhood. There should be zero crime in that area over the past several years. It is a simple enough thing to consider, but many people don't bother checking into this before buying a new home. You really don't want to be in a location where you are likely to get shot at when walking your dog in front of your house. Nor would you want to have drug dealers hanging out in front of your new home peddling their wares. Note that police presence does not necessarily make for a safe neighbourhood.

Proximity and availability of other local municipal services should also be considered. Is there regular sanitation pickup (garbage removal), or are you expected to drive your trash to the nearest landfill by yourself? How is the water supply provided, and sewers (if available)? Are the streets going to be plowed regularly (if you are in a snow area)? Usually these municipal services are paid for through real estate taxes, so ensure that you are getting a level of service for the amount of taxes that you will pay on your new home each year. If you have children and they will be attending public school, how are the schools in that area?

Last but not least, the home prices in the area must be realistic and in your price range. Naturally, the safer the neighbourhood and better the schools and municipal services, the higher the price of homes to buy. You may have to compromise on how "good" the neighbourhood is, or on the level of services available in the area, to fit within your new home buying budget. Remember the age-old golden rule: "You get what you pay for". If you want convenience, safety and services—expect to pay more for your new home in that location. Be absolutely clear about the tradeoff in safety, convenience and municipal services if you have to trade off some of these benefits to get an affordable home in the location. Your choice in location for buying a new home will stay with you for a long, long, long time.

A parking space is highly recommended. Even if you don't drive, you can always rent it out.

The last thing anyone wants to do after a hard day at work is to drive around the neighbourhood looking for a place to park. Adding a garage, driveway or other parking area to your home property is a sensible idea and a worthy investment. There are several reasons for either building or purchasing a property with off-street parking.

The parking area can add value to your home

As a matter of fact, the value such a space adds to your home can outweigh the cost of building the space. Studies have shown that one of the top ten features buyers look for when purchasing a property is a garage or off-street parking. This feature can make or break a sale. Therefore, if you do not have off-street parking at your home, consider adding a garage or driveway.

Your car is protected from damage

Many cars get damaged parking on the side of the street. Cars coming down the street misjudge the distance and can take off your side view mirror or swipe your car causing major damage. Parking your car off-street can prevent vandals from smashing your car window to steal your radio, or prevent your car from getting keyed or the tires from getting stolen.

By having parking on your property you can prevent car theft

A car parked in the garage does not provide a temptation to car thieves. Even pulling your car into a driveway or parking pad will make it less noticeable to car thieves. And a car thief has more risk going onto your property to steal your car versus taking an auto right off the street. There is less of a chance of being noticed.

Being able to park your car on your property and off the street might decrease your car insurance

Many auto insurance companies have special rates and plans for customers who can park their cars in garages on their driveways at night as opposed to parking on the street. Check with your auto insurance company for any incentives for off-street parking. You might be able to save a bundle on your insurance rates.

Having your own personal parking space in front of your home is a major convenience

By having an off-street parking space you will no longer have to drive around the neighbourhood looking for a space to park. In addition, it is much easier to unload items from your car such as grocery bags or luggage from a long trip. You will not have to double park outside your home, unload the items, and then go find a parking space. You can simply pull into your driveway or garage and unload your car.

Parking spaces in Toronto have doubled in the last ten years, which tells me that parking spaces are also a good investment, something that you can sell for a profit down the road. However, I have seen many a good house, or a good condo, become completely unsellable because there was no parking available.

Remember, when you are coming home late on Friday night with three bags of groceries, you want to park at your home. You don't want to be two blocks away still looking for a spot.

LET'S GET READY TO SELL YOUR HOME

When getting your home ready to sell, you need to look at your house in a new way. Think of your house as a product about to go on the market where it is probably competing with brand new housing. It needs to show well, which means clutter-free and well kept.

Today's home buyers lead busy lives and may not be interested in taking on major repairs or improvements upon moving in. You need to make your house a "ten". This document will help you spot what is right and what is not so good about your "product". It will give you the opportunity to take corrective action to ensure your house looks fresh, clean and well maintained when the "For Sale" sign goes up.

Get it ready

If you need to make improvements to your home, do the work before it goes on the market. Potential buyers are not interested in hearing about your good intentions to look after defects before a transfer of ownership takes places. Even if fix-up work is underway, buyers may not be able to visualize what your home will look like when the work is finished. They will just remember it being in a state of disrepair.

Should you get a pre-sale home inspection?

A serious buyer may want to have a professional home inspector check your house from top to bottom before making an offer. Even though this guide will help you identify problems on your own, the option of hiring a professional home inspector is open to you as well. If you can afford it, an inspection in advance of putting your home on the market is a good idea. It is your best way of finding and taking care of serious deficiencies before an inspector hired by potential buyers discovers them.

CMHS'S homeowner's inspection checklist

This practical, easy-to-follow guide for homeowners will help you identify common house problems and deal with them. In it, you will find illustrated how-to tips offering executive solutions for every room of your house.

• Outside

Check your house's curb appeal

How does your house look from the street? That is where prospective buyers will be when they first see your home— and that is where they will form that all-important first impression. Stand at the curb in front of your house, and note what you see.

- Remove clutter in your yard.
- Repair cracked or uneven driveway or walkway surfaces.

- If your lawn has bald spots, apply some top dressing and re-seed. Prune trees and shrubs of dead wood. Weed and mulch flower beds, if you have them. If it is the right time of year, consider buying some flower-filled planters to enhance the eye appeal of your property. Make sure your lawn is mowed regularly. Ensure that the composted area is tidy.
- Are your windows and walls clean?
- Does your front door need paint?
- Ensure your eaves and downspouts are clear of debris and in good repair.
- Are your backyard deck and walkways clean? If not, use a power washer and do any necessary painting, staining or sealing.
- If you have a swimming pool, are the deck and pool clean (when in season)?
- Do all outside lights work? Replace any burned out bulbs, and clean fixtures of dirt and cobwebs.
- Is there a shed? Does it look presentable?
- Do windows and exterior doors need recaulking? Even at six or seven years of age, the caulking may be dried out and in need of replacement.
- Do you have decorative wooden poles on the porch? Is the wood at the bottom in good condition? Overall, does it need a new coat of paint?
- If you have a gate, is it well oiled?

When you have completed the curb appeal inspection, carefully check the rest of your home's exterior.

Will your roof and chimney pass inspection?

If you are uneasy about climbing onto your roof, you can inspect most items from the ground using binoculars. Otherwise, be careful when working or moving about on your roof. Unless roof repair is a simple matter of applying new caulking, you will probably need the services of a professional.

- Check the general condition of your roof. Sagging sections, curled shingles, pooled water on flat roofs and corrosion on metal roofing means it is time for repair or replacement.
- Both masonry and metal chimneys need to be straight and structurally sound, have proper capping on top and watertight flashing where they penetrate the roof.
- All roofs undergo stress from snow and rain loads, so a truss or rafter may become damaged, resulting in a noticeable small depression. A professional should do this inexpensive repair.

Examine your walls

The condition of your exterior walls directly affects the look and curb appeal of your home.

- Replace old caulking. You may have to cut or scrape away old caulking to get a good seal. Do not seal drainage or ventilation gaps.
- Is your exterior paint looking good? If you see faded colours and cracked or peeling surfaces, you need

to repaint. Be sure to get competitive bids if you hire professional painters.

- You can clean vinyl siding, but defects or damage to it and to metal siding usually means replacement.
- Stucco can be repaired, but some skill is required to blend patches with existing stucco.

• Inside

A prospective buyer will usually enter through your front door, so that is where you should begin your interior inspection. You want your buyer to see a neat, clean, well-lit interior. Get clutter out of sight, ensure that carpets are clean and floors are scrubbed and polished, and that walls and trim show fresh paint (preferably neutral or light colours).

Take a sniff. Are there any unpleasant odours in your home? If so, track them down and eliminate them. Ensure all your lights work and are free of cobwebs. You want your home to look spacious, bright and fresh.

If you have considerable family memorabilia, consider thinning it out. Your objective is to help potential buyers feel as if they could live in your home. That mental leap becomes more difficult for them if your house resembles a shrine of your family.

Professional realtors and decorators say the most important areas of your home to upgrade and modernize are the kitchen and bathrooms. Buyers also want to see new or recently installed floor coverings throughout.

General interior

- Check stairs for loose boards, ripped carpeting, and missing or loose handrails and guards.
- Most problems with interior walls are cosmetic and can be repaired with spackling compound and paint.
- Ensure doors open and shut properly. Minor sticking is normal, but excessive binding indicates possible structural problems.
- Open and close all windows to ensure they work properly. Fogging between the panes of a sealed window indicates the seal is broken and the unit needs to be replaced.
- Keep furniture to a minimum so rooms do not appear smaller than they are. Ensure that traffic can flow in or through a room unimpeded. If they contain bookshelves or cabinets overflowing with books, magazines and knick-knacks, remove some of these items.
- Ensure closets look spacious, organized and uncluttered. Create space by getting rid of old clothes and junk.
- Remove or lock away valuables such as jewellery, coins, currency, cameras and compact discs.

Kitchen and bathrooms

- People splash water around in the kitchen and bathrooms, so check around sinks, tubs and toilets for rotting countertops and floors. Problems could be due to poor caulking or plumbing leaks. Fogged windows, molds and sweating toilet tanks indicate high humidity levels, which you can remedy with exhaust fans.
- In the kitchen, clean all appliances, including your oven. Clean or replace your greasy stove hood filter. Clean your

cabinets inside and out, as well as your countertops and backsplashes. Repair dripping faucets.

- Remove anything stored on top of your fridge, and remove artwork and magnets.
- Remove any items stored on countertops.
- Remove items stored under the sink.
- In bathrooms, scrub sinks, tubs and toilets, taking care to remove any rust stains. Remove mildew from showers and bathtubs. Fix dripping faucets or trickling toilets, and vacuum your fan grill.
- Clean mirrors, light switch plates and cupboard handles.
- Consider installing new 6-litre toilets if you currently have water-guzzlers.
- If you have ceramic tile in either your kitchen or bathroom, ensure grouting is intact and clean.

Basement

The condition of the foundation and main structural members in the basement are critical to the fitness of any house. The purpose of your inspection is to make sure these are sound and durable.

- Look for cracks, water seepage, efflorescence (white powder-like substance), crumbling mortar or concrete, and rotting wood. If any of these problems are present, you need to do further research to learn about causes and possible solutions.
- If your basement is damp or musty, consider using a dehumidifier.
- Like all other areas of your home, your basement should be organized and clutter-free.

- Change the filters in the furnace and have it cleaned. This is the number one item purchasers want done after a home inspection.
- If you have a pet with a litter box, ensure the litter box is clean.

Garage

- Get rid of the broken tools, old car parts, discarded bicycles, empty paint cans, and the hundreds of other useless items that accumulate in garages. Again, you want a clutter-free zone.
- Use cleaning solutions to remove oil stains from the floor.

LET'S LIST!

You have inspected your house and taken care of problems. Now you are ready for showings. You will need a plan of action that assigns duties to each family member so the place can quickly be whipped into shape.

- Open all drapes, blinds, etc., and turn on lights to make the house bright.
- Air out the house to get rid of cooking, pet odours, and so on.
- Have fresh flowers in view.
- Pick up clutter, and empty garbage.
- Make sure everything is spotless.
- Set your thermostat at a comfortable level.
- Remove pets from the house or put them outside.

- If you have an agent, leave when the house is being shown. If you are selling it yourself, you need to strike a balance between being helpful and crowding the buyer.
- In poor weather, provide a place for boots, overshoes and umbrellas.
- If selling in the winter months, display photos of the house in summer to show landscaping.
- Leave out heating and hydro bills.
- For those on septic system and/or well, leave out inspection and maintenance information.

Buying the right house is something you can do with a few tips and tricks to help you find what you are looking for. A lot of first-time home buyers, or consumers who are suddenly buying a home with a larger budget than expected, go out with stars in their eyes, and sometimes buy with emotion rather than with their minds. The key to this is reigning in your emotions and trying to concentrate on just a few very important and key elements to accomplish the art of buying the perfect house that suits YOU, or both yours and your partner's needs.

When choosing the right home you need to be sure of your budget. Just because the bank approves you for a larger amount than expected, does not mean that you should use the entire amount that you were approved for. Go over your budget and know exactly how much you want to spend on a house and what a comfortable monthly payment would be for you to be able to handle. If you buy something that you can afford when things are going well, consider if there is a sudden strain on finances, particularly if a spouse or partner loses their job and your income becomes the main source for a while. Could you still afford to make the house payment and afford to pay for necessities like groceries, electricity and the like? This is a very important question to ask yourself when buying a house.

Another important part to mastering the art of buying the perfect home is to reign in your emotions and concentrate on what is truly important. For example, if location is more important, try to find a house that meets your needs in your ideal area. Write a list of your needs and a few small wants that you can give to a real estate agent you trust. If you need three bedrooms and two bathrooms, but you want a bonus room or a fourth bedroom, you can list that as an optional "want" or as a "bonus" on your list. These things can go far—you can even ask for a home insurance quote in advance so you can keep that number in mind. If your real estate agent can find everything you want or need in a home but it's not in your ideal location, you need to weigh what is more important to you. Would you rather live a mile or two away from your target neighbourhood in the house of your dreams, or, in a house that may not have everything you want in your target neighbourhood? You need to decide what is more important to you and stick with that. Buy with your mind and not with your emotions.

Be sure you know exactly what you need and what your priorities are, how much you can afford to spend, and don't let your emotions get in the way (probably the best of all home buyer tips!). If you do, you may end up buying a house that is too expensive or that is pretty to look at but is impractical in maintenance or location. This is how you master the art of buying the perfect home.

SELECTING THE RIGHT REAL ESTATE AGENT

Selecting the right real estate agent can sometimes be a very long and arduous process that stresses many people out. However, if you can follow a few steps, you may find your perfect real estate agent much quicker and with a lot less stress involved. For anyone needing a real estate agent, I'm sure you would like to make it as stress-free as possible to find the perfect one for you.

First of all, it should be based on whether you are buying or selling a home. When buying a home and finding a real estate agent, you need to find someone with experience in finding homes for people in the area you are looking. Look around at the homes for sale in the neighbourhood you want to purchase in. What realtor is featured on the for sale signs? This person would be knowledgeable about the area you want to buy a home in, and can better help you find what you're looking for.

If you are selling a home, the same advice can apply. Find a realtor who has sold homes successfully in your area, and get in contact with them.

After you find some realtors that are right for you (buying or selling), you need to meet them in person. Find out about their commissions or fees, and decide whether their fees or commissions are acceptable to you. Find out if they can help you accomplish your goals in buying or selling a home. If buying, can this real estate agent help you find a house in your price range? Can this realtor accommodate your schedule if you need to view a house? Can this realtor make sure to find you a home that meets your wants or needs? If selling a home, the most important questions for your realtor would be: What is your commission if my home sells? How aggressively do you plan on marketing my home? What can you bring to the table that other realtors cannot when selling a property?

To perfect the art of finding the perfect real estate agent, you will then need to decide which realtor you want for the job. Sometimes you instantly know who will fit the bill for you. Make sure you feel comfortable with your chosen real estate agent because you will be seeing an awful lot of each other during the process, and sometimes situations can be stressful. The perfect real estate agent will make you feel comfortable, and will make you trust that they are conducting business on your behalf with the utmost character and with your best interest at heart, and not their own. Steer clear of any realtor that makes you feel as if they are more worried about how much money they will make over taking care of your needs.

When taken altogether, these steps can ensure that you are a true master in the art of finding the perfect real estate agent for you and your situation. Make sure you think everything through and pick the perfect real estate agent to ensure success in your real estate venture.

Finding a great mortgage is elusive to many first-time home buyers, or even those who have bought a home before but haven't done so in many years and do not know what current conditions are like. I'm sure everyone has heard of the mortgage crisis that has occurred in the last few years within the U.S. It has affected other countries and mortgage lenders as well. This makes it a little more confusing for home buyers shopping for the perfect mortgage for the home of their dreams.

Even though it's not quite as easy to get a mortgage now as it was several years ago, it is getting much better for the home buyer. Creditors expect you to have a better credit rating now to be considered for a home loan, and they are not as willing to offer "no money down" loans. This is what caused many of the problems. If you are serious about finding the right mortgage, you need to make sure that your credit score is decent and that you have at least a small down payment (perhaps 5 percent) to put down on your home. This will show mortgage companies that you are serious about buying a home, and they will be much more likely to offer you a better rate, which can be a considerable amount of money over the course of your loan.

You want to try and get a home mortgage loan that is fixed rate and not adjustable. An adjustable rate mortgage is usually not ideal because many of these loans seem attractive because the payments are less than a fixed rate loan, but only because these are typically low minimum payments. The minimum payment on an adjustable rate loan usually only covers the interest, and can mean you owe more on the house than the house is worth. You don't want to be in that situation. Also, interest-only payments means you are again only paying interest and nothing on the principal of the home, and with that you really aren't paying toward the principal ownership of your home at all. There are 15-year and 30-year amortized loans with an adjustable rate mortgage, which is similar to a traditional fixed rate loan except that your interest rate can change. This can cause many problems if your house payment suddenly becomes extremely expensive and out of your price range. With a fixed rate loan you know exactly how much you will be paying per month for the next twenty to thirty years, and it will not change.

While finding the best rate is important, if only half of an interest point separates a company you wholeheartedly trust to be honest with you through your home buying process, and another company that you aren't 100 percent sure about—go with the company that you wholeheartedly trust. Half of an interest point may save you a bit of money, but dealing with a company that you trust is worth its weight in gold. They will make sure and answer all of your questions, and they will make sure that the home buying process is smoother for you. When selecting a mortgage company, if there isn't one particular company that you trust, do research. Ask your friends about their home-buying experiences and mortgage companies that they used. Check with the Better Business Bureau, and research online about the mortgage company to find out if they are the type of company you want to buy a home through. These elements combined are truly the keys you need to master the art of finding the perfect mortgage. Take your time, do the research, and get the best deal you can with a company you can trust.

Selling your house for the best price is something that

takes several important key elements. This is important for you if you want to walk away with a profit or a nice hefty sum that you could potentially use to put a down payment on your new house. You have to decide on that number through weighing these key elements and coming to the best conclusion.

In order to sell for the best price, you need to look at comparables. "Comparables" is a realtor's term, and it refers to homes in your area that are similar in size, number of rooms and amenities, and how much they are being sold for. This will give you a realistic idea of what to work with. Then you need to decide what you can do to get that amount or, if you need a greater amount for your home, what you can do to your home.

Another important part of home selling for the best price is to make sure there are no repairs that need to be done. When a home is "under contract" the buyers can have a home inspection before the sale is final. If there are any costly repairs, they have the option of backing out of the purchase. Make sure there is nothing in your home that will give buyers something to worry about. Have an inspector come to your home and make sure everything is in good working order before you put your home on the market. This will ensure that the art of selling your house for the best price can be accomplished.

To truly master the art of selling your house, make sure a buyer can envision themselves in your home. If you have all of your personal pictures, oversized furniture and big screen TV, sometimes it is hard for the buyer to imagine themselves living in the house. You need to declutter your home and make sure that it is neutral so the buyers can truly envision the home and how they need it to be. If you have an office in your house, make sure that you have it set up that way so the buyer will know that is what the room is for, and they won't be confused. Another example would be if you have a breakfast nook but you have it as a playroom. The buyer may be confused. Buy or place a small table and chairs, and open up the room so the buyer knows that it is a breakfast nook. These small things are very important when trying to accomplish the art of selling your home for the best price.

These steps together, along with making sure you advertise your home with the right listing agent, and use valuable free resources of advertising your home on the Internet, will ensure that you get the best price on your home. Remember, you fell in love with your home, now bring out the best in your home so someone else can fall in love with it as well. You will walk away with a smooth selling process and more money in your pocket.

HOME STAGING

Home staging (also called house fluffing, house primping, real estate staging) is the art of decorating a home to sell quickly and for top dollar.

From recommending wall colours, repairs and decluttering, to careful arrangements of furniture, art and accessories—I'll guide you through the process to do it yourself.

Even if you're not moving, you will find these tips also make your home more relaxing and enjoyable to live in.

Successful home staging will help you sell your house sooner and possibly for more money than if you did not prepare it for selling. Remember, most people want to move into their new home without having to make updates to it.

Curb appeal

Stand back and view your home as if you were seeing it for the first time. This is the "first impression" stage. Depending on the season, you may want to have pots of colourful and attractive flowers to greet buyers, a clean and inviting door mat, new and shiny door handles and/or knockers, and a freshly painted door.

Landscaping is nice, but not in everyone's budget. At minimum, lawns should be freshly mowed, leaves raked, or snow shovelled. Consider a hanging or potted plant for the entrance. Sweep the porch, deck and all walkways, and ensure garbage and recycling are tucked neatly away from the front of the house.

Scrub your front door, porch, outside railings and steps. This is cheaper than repainting and makes a world of difference. Once the outside entrance is clean, decide if the paint really needs a touch up.

Declutter

Start your pre-pack as soon as possible. You need to decide what you are going to keep, give away, sell or throw away/recycle. Many clients will rent storage lockers or have pods delivered so they can start to clear out what is not going to make the house look good.

Pick one closet or area at a time so the task isn't as

daunting. Look at every item with a very critical eye and ask yourself why you're keeping it.

Forget about hanging onto items for a garage sale. Pick your favourite charity and donate it. You paid for these things long ago, why not just give them away to others who REALLY need them?

Clean

Most mortals can't live in a spotless environment all the time. This can be one of the more stressful aspects of having your home on the market, but it's worth the effort to sell your home for top dollar. You can hire a professional service to come in and deep clean everything; then take 20–30 minutes each day to maintain it.

Appliances should sparkle even if you're not including them with the house. After all, you might throw them in later as a negotiating tool. Counter tops, taps, sinks and bathtubs should be shiny and free of water spots.

If you have a pedestal sink, don't forget the dust that collects on top of the plumbing where it attaches to the wall. If the whole sink is spotless and the taps aren't dripping, it will look new.

Dust shelves and vacuum (or "Swiffer") the floors. Naturally, all beds should be made. At a recent open house for a home listed for over $500,000 (and over 60 days on the market), they hadn't even bothered with these two simple steps. It made you wonder what bigger things had been neglected.

Clean windows let in more light and look newer. Hire a service if you have to. It's worth the investment.

Know who to call to get your home in sparkling shape. It's all part of the home staging process.

If all this attention to detail seems over the top, think that a very clean home leaves the impression that the house is well cared for. This helps put buyers at ease— especially a first-time buyer who may be worried about the responsibilities of owning a house.

You would think a clean home is common sense, but let me assure you, I wish it was so. A clean home translates into: "They must have really cared for their home." Use environmentally friendly cleaners where you can. For hard cleaning areas, TSP is a good product. Bathrooms and kitchens must be sparkling clean at the very least.

Flowers

You don't need to spend a fortune to have fresh flowers throughout your home. Even a daisy in a bud vase brightens a bathroom counter. Ask your florist which blooms last a week. You can also use potted flowering plants that are in season for a low-cost solution.

Don't use plastic or obviously fake flowers, especially in an expensive home.

Music

Soft background music can help create a soothing environment and camouflage neighbour and traffic noise. But make sure the volume is very low. Blaring TVs are definitely a no-no, but you'd be surprised how many people leave them on for showings.

Let in some air and some light

Open some windows for at least ten minutes. There is nothing worse than walking into a stuffy house or one that smells of smoke and pet odours.

It might be mood lighting to you, but if you're trying to sell your home, keep it bright. Dimly lit rooms tend to look small and dingy, especially during the day.

If you have a particularly dark room, consider investing in a floor lamp that will bounce off the ceiling.

Spend money on new light fixtures in brushed nickel or stainless steel. Brass is out, so don't fight it. There are many low-cost lighting stores to select from, so no excuses for having dated light fixtures.

Window treatments

The most popular on the market are the 2" faux woods in a white tone to go with your trim. Decorative side panels will do the trick if you need to add warmth and colour.

Functionality

Place your furniture in each room so that you have very obvious focal points that show off the home's best selling features. If you have a beautiful fireplace, place the furniture in a parallel grouping so that the eye is drawn to the fireplace.

If you were using your guest bedroom as your den for living when selling, turn it back into a bedroom with bedroom furniture in it. If you do not have the right furniture for each room, consider renting it. There are more and more rental furnishing companies opening up every day. If you don't want to rent, then borrow.

Flooring

Tile or linoleum is great for entranceways, bathrooms, kitchens, and laundry rooms. A good quality laminate or hardwood is perfect for living rooms and family rooms. Bedrooms are attractive in a neutral carpet.

By planning and budgeting you can get yourself to the "OPEN HOUSE READY" stage.

The fact is, 79 percent of prospective buyers have already checked you out through the MLS listings. Will they like what they see?

Happy Selling!

Quick repairs

There are speedy and low cost solutions to many of the little problems that together make a home seem shabbier than it is.

Walk along each corridor and into every room, and check where your eye is drawn (better yet, ask a critical friend or family member). If the eye is drawn to the chipped white paint on the door frame, take some "white out" and fill it in. if it's those old nail holes in the wall, see if you can hang a picture to cover them.

Glue any peeling wallpaper. If it's really horrible and you can't afford the time or money to fix it properly, hang pictures and strategically place baskets. You won't cover the problem entirely (which would be wrong anyways), but you will draw your audience's attention away from the problem and onto something more visually pleasing to focus on.

Depersonalize

We know you love your family photos and your personal treasures, and for normal living they are perfect. For selling, pack them up carefully so you can showcase them in your new home. You want buyers to focus on the best features of your home, and not on your personal things or collections.

Neutral colour scheme is the way to go for selling

Choose only three colours or less to paint your house for selling. If you have an open floor plan then paint the main floor all the same colour. Bedrooms look good in light sage greens or warm blues like the new aqua.

FORMS

Analyzing forms and contracts which make up offers, listings and contracts should help clarify a very complex procedure.

Forms are created with a view to identify and satisfy general needs. The preset portion of any form is complex and can be difficult to understand. Everyone involved in a real estate transaction should be encouraged to seek and obtain professional advice to ensure a complete and accurate understanding of any form, and not rely on the explanations contained herein.

Basically there are three types of forms you will have to deal with in real estate: listing forms (which deal with listing a house or commercial property), purchasing forms (which deal with making a purchase of a house or commercial property), and lastly, representation forms (which deal with the relationship between buyers and sellers with real estate agents and companies).

LISTING FORMS

Listing Agreement: Sale

GENERAL USE: This form is a contract between a seller and a real estate company, and gives the real estate company permission to act on the seller's behalf when they offer their home for sale in the open market. A written agreement is necessary in order to secure commission and to ensure compliance with the REBBA Code of Ethics.

TOP SECTION OF THE AGREEMENT: The section at the top identifies the parties involved in the agreement and sets the timeframe for which the contract is valid. Ontario's governing body for real estate salespeople, RECO, requires the seller(s) to initial if the listing period extends beyond six months.

1. DEFINITIONS AND INTERPRETATIONS: The following section defines who will be referred to as the buyer and seller for the remainder of the document.
2. COMMISSION: The following section declares the total fee that the seller has agreed to pay to the real estate company if they are successful in selling the property. It also indicates a period of days after the expiry of the contract that the real estate company is entitled to their fee if the seller ends up selling the property privately to a buyer, who was introduced or shown to the property within the contract period. This is known as the "holdover period".
3. FINDER'S FEES: This provides consent for the salesperson to accept any finder's fee that a mortgage

company may offer to them. It also states that this fee would be collected by the salesperson in addition to the stated commission. It should be noted that a specific consent will be required at the time a finder's fee arises.

4. REPRESENTATION: The following section confirms that the salesperson has explained the different types of agency relationships that may occur in a real estate transaction. It also authorizes the real estate company to co-operate with any other real estate companies to market the seller's property, and breaks down the commission sharing structure between the parties.

5. REFERRAL OF ENQUIRIES: The following section requires the seller to work with the real estate company for the length of the contract, and states that they must inform their salesperson of any enquiry on the property that comes to the seller. If they do not inform the salesperson of an enquiry that results in a successful private sale of the property within the listing period or the holdover period, the set commission is still owed to the salesperson.

6. MARKETING: In the following section, the seller gives permission for the real estate company to place a "For Sale" and "Sold" sign on the property, and for the company to advertise it according to company policy. The seller will not be held liable for the advertising efforts of the company.

7. WARRANTY: This confirms that the people signing this agreement are all the individuals necessary to give authority to sell the property.

The provision goes on to confirm the disclosure

of third party claims such as easements, mortgages, encumbrances, and so on.

8. INDEMNIFICATION: The following section provides that salespeople cannot be held liable for the condition of the property or damages that may occur while prospective buyers view the property.

9. FAMILY LAW ACT: The following section states, in the form of a warranty, that if spousal consent was required, then the spouse has signed.

10. VERIFICATION OF INFORMATION: The following section gives the salesperson the authority to obtain and use any reasonable information regarding the property to help market the property (i.e. mortgage details, tax information).

11. USE AND DISTRIBUTION OF INFORMATION: The following section gives salespeople the right under the Privacy Act to use personal information provided to them by the seller in order to assist in making the transaction happen. It also assures the seller that this information will not be distributed to third parties (i.e. pool or moving companies).

    Because of the privacy laws, salespeople have to ask the seller if the property is not sold, would the seller give permission for other companies to call regarding the re-listing of the property after the expiry of this contract. Seller's initials are required.

12. SUCCESSORS AND ASSIGNS: This states that heirs, estate trustees or any other party legally acting on behalf of the seller must also abide by the terms of this agreement.

13. CONFLICT OR DISCREPANCY: If there are other schedules (additional information) added to this agreement by the parties involved, which contain something specific that contradicts what is in the text of the form, the information on the attachment supersedes what is on the form.

14. ELECTRONIC COMMUNICATION: This agreement, if necessary, may be sent via electronic means and still be binding on all parties.

15. SCHEDULE(S): If a specific form or document has been added to this agreement, it should be indicated here. This section states that the listing company will market the property on behalf of the seller and will endeavour to obtain an offer acceptable to the seller.

The salesperson must sign on behalf of the company.

The Declaration of Insurance is signed by the salesperson stating that they carry insurance as required by the Real Estate and Business Brokers Act (REBBA).

Listing Agreement—Commercial: Authority to Offer for Sale

GENERAL USE: This form is a contract between a seller and a real estate company that gives the real estate company permission to act on the seller's behalf when they offer their property for sale in the open market. A written agreement is necessary in order to secure commission and to ensure compliance with the REBBA Code of Ethics.

TOP SECTION OF THE AGREEMENT: The section at the top identifies the parties involved in the agreement and sets the timeframe for which the contract is valid. Ontario's governing body for real estate salespeople, RECO, requires that the seller(s) initial if the listing period extends beyond six months.

1. DEFINITIONS AND INTERPRETATIONS: The following section defines who will be referred to as the buyer and seller for the remainder of the document.

2. COMMISSION: The following section declares the total fee that the seller has agreed to pay to the real estate company if they are successful in selling the property. It also indicates a period of days, after the expiry of the contract, that the real estate company is entitled to their fee if the seller ends up selling the property privately to a buyer who was introduced or shown to the property within the contract period. This is known as the "hold-over period".

3. REPRESENTATION: The following section confirms that the salesperson has explained the different types of agency relationships that may occur in a real estate transaction. It also authorizes the real estate company to co-operate with any other real estate companies to market the seller's property, and breaks down the commission sharing structure between the parties.

4. REFERRAL OF ENQUIRIES: The following section requires the seller to work with the real estate company for the length of the contract, and states that they must inform their salesperson of any enquiry on the property

that comes to the seller. If they do not inform the salesperson of an enquiry which results in a successful private sale of the property within the listing period or holdover period, the set commission is still owed to the salesperson.

5. MARKETING: In the following section, the seller gives permission for the real estate company to place a "For Sale" and "Sold" sign on the property, and for the company to advertise it according to company policy. The seller will not be held liable for the advertising efforts of the company.

6. WARRANTY: This confirms that the people signing this agreement are all the individuals necessary to give authority to sell the property.

   The provision goes on to confirm the disclosure of third party claims such as easements, mortgages, encumbrances, and so on.

7. INDEMNIFICATION: The following section provides that salespeople cannot be held liable for the condition of the property or damages that may occur while prospective buyers view the property.

8. FAMILY LAW ACT: The following section states, in the form of a warranty, that if spousal consent was required, then the spouse has signed.

9. FINDER'S FEES: This provides consent for the salesperson to accept any finder's fee that a mortgage company may offer to them. It also states that this fee would be collected by the salesperson in addition to the stated commission. It should be noted that a specific consent will be required at the time a finder's fee arises.

10. VERIFICATION OF INFORMATION: The following section gives the salesperson the authority to obtain and use any reasonable information regarding the property to help market the property (i.e. mortgage details, tax information).

11. USE AND DISTRIBUTION OF INFORMATION: The following section gives salespeople the right under the Privacy Act to use personal information provided to them by the seller in order to assist in making the transaction happen. It also assures the seller that this information will not be distributed to third parties (i.e. pool or moving companies).

    Because of the Privacy Laws, salespeople have to ask the seller if the property is not sold, would the seller give permission for other companies to call regarding the re-listing of the property after the expiry of this contract. Seller's initials are required.

12. SUCCESSORS AND ASSIGNS: This states that heirs, estate trustees, administrators or any other party legally acting on behalf of the seller must also abide by the terms of this agreement.

13. CONFLICT OR DISCREPANCY: If there are other schedules (additional information) added to this agreement by the parties involved, which contain something specific that contradicts what is in the text of the form, the information on the attachment supersedes what is on the form.

14. ELECTRONIC COMMUNICATION: This agreement, if necessary, may be sent via electronic means and still be binding on all parties.

15. SCHEDULE(S): If a specific form or document has been added to this agreement, it should be indicated here.
    This section states that the listing company will market the property on behalf of the seller and will endeavour to obtain an offer acceptable to the seller. The salesperson must sign on behalf of the company.

The Declaration of Insurance is signed by the salesperson stating that they carry insurance as required by the Real Estate and Business Brokers Act (REBBA).

Listing Agreement—Commercial: Authority to Offer for Lease

GENERAL USE: This form is a contract between a landlord and a real estate company, which gives the real estate company permission to act on the landlord's behalf when the property for lease is in the open market. A written agreement is necessary in order to secure commission and to ensure compliance with the REBBA Code of Ethics.

TOP SECTION OF THE AGREEMENT: The section at the top identifies the parties involved in the agreement and sets the timeframe for which the contract is valid. Ontario's governing body for real estate salespeople, RECO, requires that the landlord(s) initial if the listing period extends beyond six months.

1. DEFINITIONS AND INTERPRETATIONS: The following section defines who will be referred to as the tenant and landlord for the remainder of the document.

2. COMMISSION: The following section declares the total fee that the landlord has agreed to pay to the real estate company if they are successful in leasing the property. It also indicates a period of days after the expiry of the contract that the real estate company is entitled to their fee if the landlord ends up leasing the property privately to a tenant, who was introduced or shown to the property within the contract period. This is known as the "holdover period".

3. REPRESENTATION: The following section confirms that the salesperson has explained the different types of agency relationships that may occur in a real estate transaction. It also authorizes the real estate company to co-operate with any other real estate companies to market the landlord's property, and breaks down the commission sharing structure between the parties.

4. REFERRAL OF ENQUIRIES: The following section requires the landlord to work with the real estate company for the length of the contract, and states that they must inform their salesperson of any enquiry on the property that comes to the landlord. If they do not inform the salesperson of an enquiry that results in a successful private sale of the property within the listing period or the holdover period, the set commission is still owed to the salesperson.

5. MARKETING: In the following section, the landlord gives permission for the real estate company to place a "For Lease" and "Leased" sign on the property, and for the company to advertise it according to company

policy. The landlord will not be held liable for the advertising efforts of the company

6. WARRANTY: This confirms that the people signing this agreement are all the individuals necessary to give authority to lease the property.

   The provision goes on to confirm the disclosure of third party claims such as easements, mortgages, encumbrances, and so on.

7. INDEMNIFICATION: The following section provides that salespeople cannot be held liable for the condition of the property or damages that may occur while prospective tenants view the property.

8. VERIFICATION OF INFORMATION: The following section gives the salesperson the authority to obtain and use any reasonable information regarding the property to help market the property (i.e. mortgage details, tax information).

9. USE AND DISTRIBUTION OF INFORMATION: The following section gives salespeople the right under the Privacy Act to use personal information provided to them by the landlord in order to assist in making the transaction happen. It also assures the landlord that this information will not be distributed to third parties (i.e. pool or moving companies).

   Because of the Privacy Laws, salespeople have to ask the landlord if the property is not leased, whether the landlord gives permission for other companies to call regarding the re-listing of the property after the expiry of this contract. Landlord's initials are required.

10. SUCCESSORS AND ASSIGNS: This states that heirs,

estate trustees, administrators or any other party legally acting on behalf of the landlord must also abide by the terms of this agreement.

11. CONFLICT OR DISCREPANCY: If there are other schedules (additional information) added to this agreement by the parties involved, which contain something specific that contradicts what is in the text of the form, the information on the attachment supersedes what is on the form.

12. ELECTRONIC COMMUNICATION: This agreement, if necessary, may be sent via electronic means and still be binding on all parties.

13. SCHEDULE(S): If a specific form or document has been added to this agreement, it should be indicated here.

   This section states that the listing company will market the property on behalf of the landlord and will endeavour to obtain an offer acceptable to the landlord. The salesperson must sign on behalf of the company.

The Declaration of Insurance is signed by the salesperson stating that they carry insurance as required by the Real Estate and Business Brokers Act (REBBA).

PURCHASE AGREEMENT FORMS

Agreement of Purchase and Sale: Residential Freehold

The Agreement of Purchase and Sale is the document that is used to state the buyer's desire to purchase the property, and to negotiate the terms of the sale. It is commonly referred to as an "Offer". This document also allows the buyer a chance to outline in detail all of the conditions they wish to be placed in their offer to buy the seller's property. Some common examples of a buyer's condition include arranging financing (a mortgage) for the property to be purchased, completing a home inspection, or ensuring that the sale of their current home is completed before purchasing a new one. After the offer is prepared and signed by the buyer, it is presented to the seller for acceptance. The seller, in turn, may want to make changes to the offer for the buyer to consider. This process can continue back and forth several times in an effort to reach an agreement.

1. Deposit: The buyer includes a deposit in the offer to give it authenticity and to show their sincerity to the seller. The deposit is considered part of the purchase price and is ultimately adjusted as a credit to the buyer on closing.
2. Irrevocability states the deadline that a person making an offer gives the other party to accept their Offer. If the offer is not accepted by the stated time, then the offer is over and no longer binding on any of the parties in the transaction.

3. Completion date is the date that the transaction is scheduled to be completed and, unless stated otherwise, somewhere else in the agreement, the property is to be vacant. This date is not to be on the weekend or a statutory holiday.

4. Chattels including: allows the buyer to list all the additional items separate from the property that they wish to be included in their purchase. Examples to be listed here include appliances such as "Moffat white stove" or "Hotpoint white refrigerator," perhaps with serial numbers. The seller must agree with the items included here before signing the offer. The guide to follow is: <u>when in doubt, spell it out</u>. Clear descriptions of what is expected to remain in or on the property are recommended.

5. Fixtures excluded: lists any fixtures that are attached to the property that the buyer and the seller have agreed will not be included in the deal (i.e. a chandelier in the dining room, a mirror attached to wall in front hallway, a ceiling fan. The same rule applies here as for chattels included. Specific details of the items that the seller wishes to remove on closing should be set out.

6. Rental items are items that are not included in the purchase price because they are currently being rented. An example is a hot water tank that is being rented from a utility company. Other examples (but by no means a complete list) are: alarm systems, furnaces, water softeners, and air conditioners. These are but a few. Care should be taken to ensure that all the rental items are detailed here.

7. The HST section states how HST is to be treated, if HST is to be paid.

8. Title search provides the time for the buyer's lawyer to do the necessary searches and checks on the property. These will likely include matters such as checking the title to ensure that the buyer is going to obtain good title, and that there are no outstanding work orders.

9. Future use tells the buyer that the only use the buyer can insist upon is the use set out in the agreement. If the agreement states that it is a single family home, there is no guarantee that in five years they can operate a business from the premises.

10. The title section of the agreement provides that the buyer is entitled to good title, but must accept the title subject to any easements for the supply of telephone services, electricity, gas, sewers, water, television cable facilities, and other related services. Further, the buyer has to accept the title subject to any restrictive covenants as long as they are complied with. Finally, if there are any municipal agreements, zoning bylaws or utility or service contracts, the buyer must assume them.

11. Closing arrangements sets out how the closing is to proceed, if the transaction is to be completed electronically.

12. Documents and discharge states that the seller will give the buyer any documents they have, while the buyer cannot ask for documents that the seller doesn't have. When there is a mortgage on the property in favour of a bank, trust company, insurance company, credit union or Caisse Populaire—in most instances a discharge is

not available for registration on closing. This paragraph sets out the procedure for dealing with these matters. A mortgage other than those set out above must be paid out and discharged on closing.

13. Inspection makes it known that the buyer has had the opportunity to do a personal inspection of the property they are purchasing. The buyer also acknowledges that, unless it is stated in the body of the offer, they declined the opportunity to have a professional home inspection completed on the property.

14. The insurance clause states that the seller must take care of the property until closing, and is responsible to maintain fire insurance policies, if any, on the property until closing. If there is a fire before closing, the buyer has two choices: They can either not buy the property, or they can have insurance money paid to them and take the property as it is.

15. The agreement is subject to compliance with the Planning Act. This statute governs things like severance.

16. Document preparation spells out that the buyer will take responsibility to pay for the preparation of their own mortgages and the Land Transfer Tax Affidavit. The seller, meanwhile, is responsible for preparing a deed to transfer at the seller's expense.

17. The residency paragraph deals with the issue of the seller's residency in Canada. It ensures that the seller is a resident of Canada, or if they are a non-resident, that they have paid any taxes owed payable under the non-residency provisions of the Income Tax Act.

18. The adjustments section states that certain charges

applicable to the property, such as property taxes or utilities, will be adjusted on the completion day. The buyer will assume responsibility beginning on the day of the completion of the sale.

19. The property may be re-evaluated on an annual basis. Buyer and seller agree that change may take place and salespeople cannot be held responsible for any changes.

20. All deadlines must be met according to the dates and times stated in the agreement.

21. Tender states that in order to demonstrate that a party is ready, willing and able to complete a transaction, a party must produce certain items. For the buyer it is generally money, for the seller it will include things like a transfer/deed and keys. This paragraph sets out how each party performs their side.

22. The Family Law Act states that no spouse has a claim to this property other than a spouse who consented to the contract in the signature as set aside for that purpose.

23. The seller warrants that while living on the property they have not used insulation containing urea-formaldehyde (UFFI). Further, the seller is not aware of that kind of insulation ever having been used on the property.

24. Any advice given by the brokerage in regards to these conditions is not to be considered an expert opinion. If these factors impact the transaction or property valuation, seek the advice of an independent professional.

25. The consumer reports section notifies the seller that a personal or credit check may be obtained on the buyer.

26. If there is any conflict or discrepancy between the

preset portion of the form and any provision added, then the added provision will supersede the preset portion. The following paragraph also confirms that no other agreements have been made other than what is contained in this agreement.

27. Any time and date stated on the agreement is based on the time where the property is located.

28. In the event one of the parties to the agreement dies, the successors and assigns paragraph states their heirs or executors are bound by the agreement.

Agreement of Purchase and Sale: Condominium Resale

GENERAL USE: The Agreement of Purchase and Sale Condominium Resale is the document that is used to state the buyer's desire to purchase the property, and to negotiate the terms of the sale. It is commonly referred to as an "Offer". This document also allows the buyer a chance to outline in detail all of the conditions they wish to be placed in their offer to buy the seller's property. Some common examples of a buyer's conditions include: arranging financing (a mortgage) for the property to be purchased, completing a home inspection, ensuring that the sale of their current home is completed before purchasing a new one or review of a Status Certificate. After the offer is prepared and signed by the buyer, it is presented to the seller for acceptance. The seller, in turn, may want to make changes to the offer for the buyer to consider. This process can continue back and forth several times in an effort to reach an agreement.

1. DEPOSIT: The buyer includes a deposit in the offer to give it authenticity and to show their sincerity to the seller. The deposit is considered part of the purchase price and is ultimately adjusted as a credit to the buyer on closing.

2. IRREVOCABILITY: The following section states the deadline that a person making an offer gives the other party to accept their offer. If the offer is not accepted by the stated time, then the offer is over and no longer binding on any of the parties involved in the transaction.

3. COMPLETION DATE: This is the date that the transaction is scheduled to be completed, and unless stated otherwise somewhere else in the agreement, the property is to be vacant. This date is not to be on the weekend or a statutory holiday.

4. NOTICES: In order to accomplish the terms of an agreement, various notices need to be given. This paragraph sets out the different options available in order to effect notice.

5. CHATTELS INCLUDED: The following section allows the buyer to list all additional items separate from the property that they wish to be included in their purchase. Examples to be listed here include appliances such as "Moffat white stove" or "Hotpoint white refrigerator," perhaps with serial numbers. The seller must agree with items included before signing the offer. The guide to follow is: <u>when in doubt spell it out</u>. Clear descriptions of what is expected to remain in or on the property are recommended.

6. FIXTURES EXCLUDED: The following section lists

any fixtures that are attached to the property that the buyer and the seller have agreed will not be included in the deal (i.e. a chandelier in the dining room, a mirror attached to wall in the front hallway). The same rule applies here as for chattels included. Specific details of the items that the seller wishes to remove on closing should be set out.

7. RENTAL ITEMS: The following section deals with items that are not included in the purchase price because they are currently being rented. An example is a hot water tank that is being rented from a utility company. Other examples (but by no means a complete list) are: alarm systems, furnaces, water softeners, air conditioners. These are but a few. Care should taken to ensure that all the rental items are detailed here.

   The buyer agrees to assume any rental contracts, for example, a rental contract for the hot water tank, if assumable.

8. COMMON EXPENSES: These are expenses that are charged to an owner, generally collected monthly, on account of operating, management, maintenance and repairs. Details of what is included in these expenses are usually found in a schedule to the Declaration of the Condominium.

9. PARKING AND LOCKERS: Parking spaces and lockers are usually detailed at the beginning of the Agreement of Purchase and Sale. If the parking spaces and/or lockers are assigned and not detailed at the beginning, their description will be noted here if there are additional common expenses or costs payable.

10. HST: The following section states how HST is to be treated, if HST is to be paid.
11. TITLE SEARCH: The following section provides the times for the buyer's lawyer to do the necessary searches and checks on the property.

    These will likely include matters such as checking the title to ensure that the buyer is going to obtain good title, and that there are no outstanding work orders.
12. TITLE: This paragraph provides that the buyer is entitled to good title but must accept the title subject to any easements for the supply of telephone services, electricity, gas, sewers, water, television cable facilities and other related services. Further, the buyer has to accept the title subject to any restrictive covenants as long as they are complied with. Since this is a condominium, the buyer agrees to accept the property subject to the provisions of the Condominium Act, its regulations as well as the terms and conditions in the declaration, rules and bylaws. Finally, if there are any municipal agreements, zoning bylaws, utility or service contracts, the buyer must assume them.
13. CLOSING ARRANGEMENTS: If the transaction is to be completed electronically, the following paragraph sets out how the closing is to proceed.
14. STATUS CERTIFICATE AND MANAGEMENT OF CONDOMINIUM: A Status Certificate is meant to set out the current status of the Condominium Corporation. It will include additional documents such as financial statements, budgets, reserve fund audits, declaration, rules, bylaws, to name a few. The seller consents to the buyer

obtaining a Status Certificate. This paragraph provides warranties that there are no special assessments or legal actions pending or contemplated.

15. DOCUMENTS AND DISCHARGE: The following paragraph states that the seller will give the buyer any documents they have, while the buyer cannot ask for documents that the seller doesn't have. When there is a mortgage on the property in favour of a bank, trust company, insurance company, credit union or Caisse Populaire—in most instances a discharge is not available for registration on closing. This paragraph sets out the procedure for dealing with these matters. A mortgage other than those set out above must be paid out and discharged on closing.

16. MEETINGS: Seller must advise prospective buyer if the seller has received notice of a meeting: (a) that status of condo will not continue, (b) that no major renovations are planned, (c) or any major changes to finances of the Condominium Corporation. If any occur before closing, the buyer must be told, and will have the option to terminate the agreement.

17. INSPECTION: The following paragraph makes it known that the buyer has had the opportunity to do a personal inspection of the property they are purchasing. The buyer also acknowledges that, unless it is stated in the body of the offer, the buyer declined the opportunity to have a professional home inspection completed on the property.

18. APPROVAL OF THE AGREEMENT: If it is necessary to obtain consent to the transaction from the

Condominium Corporation or its Board of Directors, then the seller agrees to apply immediately for the consent. If the necessary consent is not received, then the transaction is at an end.

19. INSURANCE: The following paragraph provides that the seller is responsible for the property until closing. If there is substantial damage to the property, the buyer has one of two choices. One is permit the proceeds of insurance to be used to repair the damage in accordance with the Condominium's Insurance Trust Agreement; or two, end the transaction.

20. DOCUMENT PREPARATION: This spells out that the buyer will take responsibility to pay for the preparation of their own mortgages and the Land Transfer Tax Affidavit. The seller, meanwhile, is responsible for preparing a deed to transfer at the seller's expense.

21. RESIDENCY: The following paragraph deals with the issue of the seller's residency in Canada. It ensures that the seller is a resident of Canada, or if they are a non-resident that they have paid any taxes owed payable under the non-residency provisions of the Income Tax Act.

22. ADJUSTMENTS: The following section states that certain charges applicable to the property, such as common expenses, property taxes or utilities, will be adjusted on the completion day. The buyer will assume responsibility beginning on the day of the completion of the sale.

23. PROPERTY ASSESSMENT: The property may be re-evaluated on an annual basis. Buyer and seller agree

that change may take place and salespeople cannot be held responsible for any changes.

24. TIME LIMITS: All deadlines must be met according to the dates and times stated in this agreement.

25. TENDER: In order to demonstrate that a party is ready, willing and able to complete a transaction, a party must produce certain items. For the buyer it is generally money, for the seller it will include things like a transfer/deed and keys. This paragraph sets out how each party performs their side.

26. FAMILY LAW ACT: The following section states that no spouse has a claim to this property other than a spouse who consented to the contract in the signature area set aside for that purpose.

27. UFFI: The seller warrants that while living on the property they have not used insulation containing urea-formaldehyde. Further, the seller is not aware of that kind of insulation ever having been used on the property.

28. LEGAL, ACCOUNTING AND ENVIRONMENTAL ADVICE: Any advice given by the brokerage in regards to these conditions is not to be considered an expert opinion. If these factors impact the transaction or property valuation, seek the advice of an independent professional.

29. CONSUMER REPORTS: The following section notifies the buyer that a personal or credit check may be obtained on the buyer.

30. AGREEMENT IN WRITING: If there is any conflict or discrepancy between the preset portion of the form

and any provision added, then the added provision will supersede the preset portion. The following paragraph also confirms that no further agreements have been made other than what is contained in this agreement.

31. TIME AND DATE: Any time and date stated on this agreement is based on the time where the property is located.

32. SUCCESSORS AND ASSIGNS: In the event one of the parties to the agreement dies, their heirs or executors are bound by the agreement.

Agreement of Purchase and Sale: Commercial

GENERAL USE: The Agreement of Purchase and Sale is the document that is used to state the buyer's desire to purchase the property, and to negotiate the terms of the sale. It is commonly referred to as an "Offer". This document also allows the buyer a chance to outline in detail all of the conditions they wish to be placed in their offer to buy the seller's property. After the offer is prepared and signed by the buyer, it is presented to the seller for acceptance. The seller, in turn, may want to make changes to the offer for the buyer to consider. This process can continue back and forth several times in an effort to reach an agreement.

1. DEPOSIT: The buyer includes a deposit in the offer to give it authenticity and to show their sincerity to the seller. The deposit is considered part of the purchase price and is ultimately adjusted as a credit to the buyer on closing.

2. IRREVOCABILITY: The following section states the deadline that a person making an offer gives the other party to accept their offer. If the offer is not accepted by the stated time, then the offer is over and no longer binding on any of the parties in the transaction.

3. COMPLETION DATE: This is the date that the transaction is scheduled to be completed, and unless stated otherwise, somewhere else in the agreement, the property is to be vacant. This date is not to be on the weekend or a statutory holiday.

4. NOTICES: In order to accomplish the terms of an agreement, various notices need to be given. This paragraph sets out the different options available in order to effect notice.

5. CHATTELS INCLUDED: The following section allows the buyer to list all additional items separate from the property that they wish to be included in their purchase. Examples to be listed here include items such as "Mitsubishi forklift" or "Bosch cafeteria fridge," perhaps with serial numbers. The seller must agree with items included before signing the offer. The guide to follow is: <u>when in doubt spell it out</u>. Clear descriptions of what is expected to remain in or on the property are recommended.

6. FIXTURES EXCLUDED: The following section lists any fixtures that are attached to the property that the buyer and the seller have agreed will not be included in the deal (i.e. a lighting system in the lobby, a mirror attached to wall in boardroom). The same rule applies here as for chattels included. Specific details of the

items that the seller wishes to remove on closing should be set out.

7. RENTAL ITEMS: In the following section, specify if any items such as vending machines are owned by third parties, with the buyer assuming the remainder of the rental contract with the vending machine supplier.

8. HST: The following section states how HST is to be treated, if HST is to be paid.

9. TITLE SEARCH: The following section provides the times for the buyer's lawyer to do the necessary searches and checks on the property. These will likely include matters such as checking the title to ensure that the buyer is going to obtain good title, and that there are no outstanding work orders.

10. FUTURE USE: The buyer is being told that the only use the buyer can insist upon is the use(s) set out in the agreement. If the agreement states "industrial" as the only designated use, there is no guarantee that in five years the buyer can use the property for retail or residential.

11. TITLE: This paragraph provides that the buyer is entitled to good title, but must accept the title subject to any easements for the supply of telephone services, electricity, gas, sewers, water, television cable facilities and other related services. Further, the buyer has to accept the title subject to any restrictive covenants as long as they are complied with. Finally, if there are any municipal agreements, zoning bylaws or utility or service contracts, the buyer must assume them.

12. CLOSING ARRANGEMENTS: If the transaction is to be

completed electronically, the following paragraph sets out how the closing is to proceed.

13. DOCUMENTS AND DISCHARGE: The following paragraph states that the seller will give the buyer any documents they have, while the buyer cannot ask for documents that the seller doesn't have. When there is a mortgage on the property in favour of a bank, trust company, insurance company, credit union or Caisse Populaire—in most instances a discharge is not available for registration on closing. This paragraph sets out the procedure for dealing with these matters. A mortgage other than those set out above must be paid out and discharged on closing.

14. INSPECTION: The following paragraph makes it known that the buyer has had the opportunity to do a personal inspection of the property they are purchasing. The buyer also acknowledges that, unless it is stated in the body of the offer, the buyer declined the opportunity to have a professional property inspection completed on the property.

15. INSURANCE: The following clause states that the seller must take care of the property until closing, and is responsible to maintain fire insurance policies, if any, on the property until closing. If there is a fire before closing, the buyer has two choices: They can either not buy the property, or they can have insurance money paid to them and take the property as it is.

16. PLANNING ACT: The following paragraph states that the agreement is subject to compliance with the Planning Act. This statute governs issues such as severance.

17. DOCUMENT PREPARATION: This spells out that the buyer will take responsibility to pay for the preparation of their mortgages and the Land Transfer Tax Affidavit. The seller, meanwhile, is responsible for preparing a deed to transfer at the seller's expense.

18. RESIDENCY: The following paragraph deals with the issue of the seller's residency in Canada. It ensures that the seller is a resident of Canada, or if they are a non-resident, they have paid any taxes owed payable under the non-residency provisions of the Income Tax Act.

19. ADJUSTMENTS: The following section states that certain charges applicable to the property, such as property taxes or utilities, will be adjusted on the completion day. The buyer will assume responsibility beginning on the day of the completion of the sale.

20. TIME LIMITS: All deadlines must be met according to the dates specified in this agreement. However, based on written consent between the buyer and seller, these dates may be modified.

21. PROPERTY ASSESSMENT: The property may be re-evaluated on an annual basis. Buyer and seller agree that change may take place and salespeople cannot be held responsible for any changes.

22. TENDER: In order to demonstrate that a party is ready, willing and able to complete a transaction, a party must produce certain items. For the buyer it is generally money, for the seller it will include things like a transfer/deed and keys. This paragraph sets out how each party performs their side.

23. FAMILY LAW ACT: The following section states that no

spouse has a claim to this property other than a spouse who consented to the contract in the signature area set aside for that purpose.

24. UFFI: The seller warrants that while owning the property, they have not used insulation containing urea-formaldehyde. Further, the seller is not aware of that kind of insulation ever having been used on the property.

25. LEGAL, ACCOUNTING AND ENVIRONMENTAL ADVICE: Any advice given by the brokerage in regards to these conditions is not to be considered an expert opinion. If these factors impact the transaction or property valuation, seek the advice of an independent professional.

26. CONSUMER REPORTS: The following section notifies the buyer that a personal or credit check may be obtained on the buyer and/or their company.

27. AGREEMENT IN WRITING: If there is any conflict or discrepancy between the preset portion of the form and any provision added, then the added provision will supersede the preset portion. The following paragraph also confirms that no other agreements have been made other than what is contained in this agreement.

28. TIME AND DATE: Any time and date stated on this agreement is based on the time where the property is located.

29. SUCCESSORS AND ASSIGNS: In the event one of the parties to the agreement dies, their heirs or executors are bound by the agreement.

REPRESENTATION FORMS

Buyer Customer Service Agreement

When selling a home, most people are aware they sign a Listing Agreement with a realtor. There is, however, an agreement that realtors ask their home-buying clients to sign. It's an agreement that works in favour of buyers, guaranteeing the very best in real estate service.

RECO introduced guiding principles mandating that realtors ask their clients to sign a Written Representation Agreement at the earliest possible time.

When choosing representation, home buyers have the option to sign either a Buyer Representation Agreement or a Buyer Customer Service Agreement. The Buyer Representation Agreement signifies that for a designated period of time, the buyer has engaged a specific realtor firm to work exclusively on their behalf at finding a property. The agreement confirms the realtor's commitment to ensure best efforts for the buyer.

By signing the Buyer Customer Service Agreement, the buyer acknowledges that the broker has provided them with written information explaining agency relationships, including seller representation, sub-agency, buyer representation, multiple representation and customer service.

The Buyer Customer Service Agreement is used when a buyer is not a client, but rather a customer.

1. The definitions and interpretations section defines who will be referred to as the buyer and seller for the remainder of the document.
2. The buyer customer does not pay commission unless otherwise agreed to in writing.
3. The representation and customer service section confirms that the salesperson has explained the different types of agency relationships that may occur in a real estate transaction. It also confirms that the buyer falls under customer status and that the salesperson does not represent the buyer as a client. It also outlines that the salesperson must treat the buyer fairly and honestly, answer the buyer's questions with due care, and cannot purposely misrepresent the buyer.
4. Indemnification provides that salespeople cannot be held liable for the conditions of the property or damages that may occur while prospective buyers view the property.
5. Finder's fee provides consent for the salesperson to accept a fee that a mortgage company may offer to them. It also states that this fee would be collected by the salesperson in addition to the stated commission. It should be noted that a specific consent will be required at the time a finder's fee arises.
6. Consumer reports state that the buyer understands that credit checks and personal information about them may be used in the process of them purchasing a property.
7. Use and distribution of information gives salespeople the right under the Privacy Act to use personal

information provided to them by the buyer in order to assist in making the transaction happen. It also assures the buyer that this information will not be distributed to third parties (i.e. pool or moving companies).

8. If there are other schedules (additional information) added to this agreement by the parties involved, which contain something specific that contradicts what is in the text of the form, the information on the attachment supersedes what is on the form.

9. This agreement, if necessary, may be sent via electronic means, and still be binding on all parties.

10. The final section states that the company providing customer service to the buyer will assist the buyer in locating a property of a general description, as indicated above, and endeavour to obtain an offer for the buyer.

Buyer Representation Agreement Intro

If you're looking at a buyer representation (agency) agreement only as protection for the real estate agent or broker, you're missing a good deal of its value. There are significant values that can accrue to the buyer client as well. If you have trouble broaching the subject with buyers or asking for a signature on this document, here's some help.

1. *The buyer is assured of your best efforts*
    If a buyer is working with multiple agents, or they're out cruising the open houses, you are at risk of losing them at any time. It's only logical that you would have a significantly higher level of comfort with a representation agreement, and thus you'd be willing

to spend more time and effort in scouring the market for the right properties for your buyer clients. To help you put this in front of your buyer prospect in a positive way, you might say that you do a pre-showing drive-by of properties for your agreement clients. Due to the time and expense requirements, you are unable to offer this to non-clients.

2. *Your buyer representation clients are exposed to every eligible property*
This is a big one for them. If this doesn't get them into the mode to sign the agreement, then nothing else is likely to do so. This might also indicate a less-than-serious buyer. Basically:

> "Mr. & Mrs. Buyers, I am aware of some properties that might possibly meet your requirements but are not listed in the MLS. I feel it's in your best interests, and my duty, to look for FSBO properties that you might want to see. But we'll need to agree that I'll get paid a minimum commission if one of these properties turns out to be the right one for you. You can negotiate its payment as part of the transaction."

3. *Last, but not least: You get paid for sure*
This one is for your mental and financial comfort level. It's a whole lot nicer going to the office each day knowing that you'll be showing properties to buyers who are serious enough to guarantee that you'll get paid. There's also that better feeling you'll get from knowing that you were able to show them all the homes that met their requirements, as well as having them well-informed as

to their choices in representation. It's not fun having a buyer ask you after a purchase why they didn't see the home three streets over at a better price.

Buyer Representation Agreement

The Buyer Representation Agreement is a contract between a buyer and a real estate company that gives the real estate company permission to act on the buyer's behalf in the purchase of a property. Assuming the buyer is a client of the real estate company, the Real Estate Council of Ontario REBBA (Real Estate and Business Brokers Act) Code of Ethics requires that salespeople have a written Buyer Representation Agreement presented for signature prior to an offer being presented on behalf of the buyer.

The section at the top identifies the parties involved in the agreement, and sets the timeframe for which the contract is valid. The REBBA Code of Ethics requires the buyer's initials on this form if the agreement is to extend beyond six months.

Geographic location indicates the area agreed upon by both the buyer and the real estate company, for which the agreement is valid. It is usually the area in which the buyer wishes to purchase a property.

This statement affirms that the buyer has not signed a contract of this nature with any other real estate company.

The buyer hereby warrants that the buyer is not party to a Buyer Representation Agreement with any other registered real estate brokerage for the purchase or lease of a real property of the general description indicated above.

1. The first section, definitions and interpretations, defines who will be referred to as the buyer and seller for the remainder of the document.
2. The commission section establishes the commission structure for the process. It states that the buyer understands that the real estate company (salesperson) will be paid a fee by the company that has the property listed. If the buyer indicates in the commission portion to pay the real estate company a specific amount, and the portion offered by the company listing the property is less than what the buyer has agreed to pay, then the buyer is responsible for the difference. The buyer is to be informed of the commission amount being paid by the company with whom the property is listed.
3. Representation confirms that the salesperson has explained the different types of agency relationships that may occur in a real estate transaction.
4. The referral of properties requires the buyer to commit to work with the real estate company for the length of the contract, and states that they must inform their salesperson if they become aware of a property of interest to them. If they do not inform the salesperson of a property of interest that they subsequently purchase on their own, the set commission will still be owed to the salesperson.

Sections 5 through 10 of this agreement are the same as sections 4 through 9 of the Buyer Customer Service Agreement.

11. If a specific form or document has been added to this agreement, it should be indicated in the schedules section. This section states that the company representing the buyer will assist the buyer in locating a property with a general description as indicated above, and endeavour to obtain the acceptance of an offer for the buyer.

   The salesperson must sign on behalf of the company representing the buyer.

The declaration of insurance is signed by the salesperson stating that they carry insurance as required by REBBA.

Confirmation of Co-operation and Representation

GENERAL USE: This form is used to indicate to all parties involved the specific types of relationships that exist.

This document is used in part to reassure all parties that they will be treated fairly in the transaction. The form is used to set up an arrangement between companies, and is acknowledged by the parties.

DECLARATION OF INSURANCE: The Real Estate and Business Brokers Act (REBBA) that governs practitioners requires them to declare in writing to all buyers and sellers that they are insured.

a) The following option indicates that the seller is being represented by a salesperson from the listing company, and the buyer is a customer.

b) The following option is for multiple representation, and states that the listing company represents both the seller and the buyer in the transaction, and needs their consent. It also states that any conversations between the company representatives and the buyers or sellers regarding money (or their motivation for buying or selling) will be kept confidential if the parties so wish.

The following option is used only when a buyer requests a salesperson from the real estate company to represent them in the process of purchasing a property that is not listed for sale.

(A)

(1) This option indicates that the buyer is being represented by a salesperson or broker from a real estate company, and that the listing company will pay the buyer's company a commission as stated on the MLS system.

(2) This option states that the buyer is being represented by a salesperson or broker from a real estate company, the property is not listed on the MLS system, and the listing company will pay the buyer's company a commission.

(3) This option indicates that the buyer is being represented by a salesperson or broker from a real estate company, and that the buyer's company will be paid directly by the buyer.

(4) This option allows the co-operating company to indicate that the seller is paying the commission as outlined in the Commission Agreement Form.

(B)

(1) This option indicates that the buyer's company is not representing either the buyer or the seller, and that

the listing company will pay the buyer's company a commission as stated on the MLS system.

(2) This option indicates that the buyer's company is not representing either the buyer or the seller, the property is not listed on the MLS system, and the listing company will pay the buyer's company a commission.

(3) This option allows the co-operating company to indicate that the seller is paying the commission as outlined in the Commission Agreement Form.

COMMISSION TRUST AGREEMENT: The following area is for the salespeople to use regarding which trust accounts the commissions for the transaction will be paid from.

Seller Customer Service Agreement: Commission Agreement for Property Not Listed

GENERAL USE: This form is a contract between a seller and a real estate company that gives the real estate company permission to act on the seller's behalf when they offer their home for sale in the open market. A written agreement is necessary in order to secure commission and to ensure compliance with the REBBA Code of Ethics.

TOP SECTION OF THE AGREEMENT: The section at the top identifies the parties involved in the agreement, and sets the timeframe for which the contract is valid. RECO requires that the seller(s) initial if the listing period extends beyond six months.

1. DEFINITIONS AND INTERPRETATIONS: The following section defines who will be referred to as the buyer and seller for the remainder of the document.

2. COMMISSION: The following section declares the total fee that the seller has agreed to pay to the real estate company if they are successful in selling the property. It also indicates a period of days after the expiry of the contract that the real estate company is entitled to their fee if the seller ends up selling the property privately to a buyer, who was introduced or shown to the property within the contract period. This is known as the "holdover period".

3. REPRESENTATION AND CUSTOMER SERVICE: The following section confirms that the salesperson has explained the different types of agency relationships that may occur in a real estate transaction. It also authorizes the real estate company to co-operate with any other real estate companies to market the seller's property, and breaks down the commission sharing structure between the parties.

4. DEPOSIT: The buyer includes a deposit in the offer to give it authenticity and to show their sincerity to the seller. The deposit is considered part of the purchase price and is ultimately deducted from the proceeds on closing.

5. FINDER'S FEES: This provides consent for the salesperson to accept any finder's fee that a mortgage company may offer to them. It also states that this fee would be collected by the salesperson in addition to the stated commission. It should be noted that a specific consent will be required at the time a finder's fee arises.

6. INSURANCE: The seller warrants that the property is insured, including personal liability insurance.

7. VERIFICATION OF INFORMATION: The following section gives the salesperson the authority to obtain and use any reasonable information regarding the property to help market the property (i.e. mortgage details, tax information).

8. USE AND DISTRIBUTION OF INFORMATION: The following section gives salespeople the right under the Privacy Act to use personal information provided to them by the seller in order to assist in making the transaction happen. It also assures the seller that this information will not be distributed to third parties (i.e. pool or moving companies).

9. FAMILY LAW ACT: The following section states, in the form of a warranty, that if spousal consent was required, then the spouse has signed.

10. SUCCESSORS AND ASSIGNS: This states that heirs, estate trustees or any other party legally acting on behalf of the seller must also abide by the terms of this agreement.

11. CONFLICT OR DISCREPANCY: If there are other schedules (additional information) added to this agreement by the parties involved, which contain something specific that contradicts what is in the text of the form, the information on the attachment supersedes what is on the form.

12. ELECTRONIC COMMUNICATION: This agreement, if necessary, may be sent via electronic means and still be binding on all parties.

13. SOLD SIGN: The seller consents that when the property is sold, the brokerage is allowed to put a "Sold" sign on the property.

14. SCHEDULE(S): If a specific form or document has been added to this agreement, this section states that the company representing the seller will assist the seller and endeavour to obtain an acceptable offer for the seller.

The declaration of insurance is signed by the salesperson stating that they carry insurance as required by the Real Estate and Business Brokers Act (REBBA).

I hope the explanation of these forms makes real estate, and the purchasing and selling of such, a little easier to understand. But trusting the right agent will put you on the right track.

Afterword

In summary, I guess the industry that I am in is one of the most emotional and personal ones that there are.

You see, I don't sell houses, I sell homes. Houses are bricks and mortar. Homes are special. They are where we celebrate births, birthdays and Christmas. It's where we mourn the loss of a family member or a friend. It's where we met our best friend forever, down the street. It's where we won the Stanley Cup 647 times.

I still visit my old neighbourhood where I was raised, and I never thought of it as a short-term investment. I thought of it as a home.

So go ahead, buy that home and start some new dreams and memories. And when those dreams have become memories, you will look back and realize that it was also a great investment.

Thank you for reading my book.